Praise for

FOCUS

"Dr. Shojai cuts through the static to help you focus your life on the things that are specifically most important to you. His step-by-step plan for having your focus and intention guide you will bring fulfillment and satisfaction with the choices you make and the life you lead. If you want to be healthy and full of life, you'll need an operating system that supports those decisions each day. This book will help you do just that."

— **Mark Hyman, M.D.**, *New York Times* best-selling author of *Food*; *Eat Fat, Get Thin*; and *The Blood Sugar Solution*

"Do you know where you put your energy? If not, how are you going to get the life you want? This book gives you the plan and the energy budget you need to get there."

— **Dave Asprey**, *New York Times* best-selling author of *The Bulletproof Diet*

"We all know what we need to do but simply don't follow through with it. *Focus* is the missing ingredient in the health world we've been waiting for. With this mind-body framework, Dr. Shojai elegantly lays out a roadmap to success that's easy to follow and very effective. I highly recommend this book."

— **JJ Virgin**, nutrition expert and *New York Times* best-selling author of *The Virgin Diet*

"Becoming an optimal performer means having a mental operating system that is focused, drives you forward, and creates a framework for success. How do we organize our lives to actually do just that? Pedram has cracked the code and solved that riddle in a powerful way. Willpower alone won't get you there. But there is a Holy Grail that Dr. Shojai shares in *Focus*. This book is a must-read."

— **Ben Greenfield**, founder of Ben Greenfield Fitness and Kion and *New York Times* best-selling author of *Boundless*

"Everyone wants to be a 10 in life, where health equals 10, abundance equals 10, and relationships equal 10. But reality is often a downer. Our birthright is to live a life full of vitality, vigor, and abundant energy. But often our day-to-day has gotten in the way. Whether you want to increase your number, up your game, or biohack your life, *Focus* is an excellent guide."

— **Tom O'Bryan, D.C., CCN, DACBN**, author of *The Autoimmune Fix*

FOCUS

BY NICK POLIZZI
AND PEDRAM SHOJAI, O.M.D.

Exhausted

All of the above are available at your local bookstore,
or may be ordered by visiting:

Hay House USA: www.hayhouse.com®
Hay House Australia: www.hayhouse.com.au
Hay House UK: www.hayhouse.co.uk
Hay House India: www.hayhouse.co.in

***

FOCUS

BRINGING TIME, ENERGY, AND MONEY INTO FLOW

PEDRAM SHOJAI, O.M.D.

HAY HOUSE, INC.
Carlsbad, California • New York City
London • Sydney • New Delhi

Published in the United States by: Hay House, Inc.: www.hayhouse
.com® • **Published in Australia by:** Hay House Australia Pty. Ltd.: www
.hayhouse.com.au • **Published in the United Kingdom by:** Hay House UK,
Ltd.: www.hayhouse.co.uk • **Published in India by:** Hay House Publishers
India: www.hayhouse.co.in

Cover design: Ploy Siripant • *Interior design:* Nick C. Welch

The author of this book does not dispense medical advice or prescribe
the use of any technique as a form of treatment for physical, emotional,
or medical problems without the advice of a physician, either directly or
indirectly. The intent of the author is only to offer information of a general nature to help you in your quest for emotional, physical, and spiritual
well-being. In the event you use any of the information in this book for
yourself, the author and the publisher assume no responsibility for your
actions.

Library of Congress has cataloged the earlier edition as follows:

Names: Shojai, Pedram, author.
Title: Focus : bringing time, energy, and money into flow / Pedram Shojai,
   O.M.D.
Identifiers: LCCN 2020034394 | ISBN 9781401960377 (hardback) | ISBN
   9781401960384 (ebook)
Subjects: LCSH: Time management. | Self-actualization (Psychology) |
   Mindfulness (Psychology)
Classification: LCC HD69.T54 S56 2020 | DDC 650.1--dc23
LC record available at https://lccn.loc.gov/2020034394

Tradepaper ISBN: 978-1-4019-6222-7
E-book ISBN: 978-1-4019-6038-4
Audiobook ISBN: 978-1-4019-6063-6

10 9 8 7 6 5 4 3 2 1
1st edition, November 2020
2nd edition, December 2021

Printed in the United States of America

To Elmira, Sol, and Sophia.
All of my love . . . always.

CONTENTS

CHAPTER ONE

LIFE

Life is a funny thing. We never really stop to think about it because we're too busy living it.

Living life.

There are lots of people doing that . . . well, kind of.

People are eating, sleeping, working, procreating, and driving. They are getting news on their phones, binge-watching shows, and drinking coffee to get through their days.

They are hustling to make a living, looking forward to vacations, and pushing their kids to buy into that same narrative so they can work hard and have a better life.

I guess we can call all of that "living life," but let's take a moment and examine the root of these two words: *live* and *life*.

Live (the root of *living*)—the primary definition in the dictionary for this is "to remain alive."

At first glance it seems like a pretty low bar, but let's think about it. The statement implies an incredibly miraculous symphony of trillions of biological functions that have to work together in harmony and symbiosis with the trillions of other life forms around us to keep our bodies humming. It doesn't account for the "spark of life" or consciousness that imbues this meat suit that keeps the lights on, or at the very least is somehow *aware* that we're alive.

This definition puts mere survival at center stage for us and, to be fair, that was the dominant theme for our species for centuries, before we got smarter and richer. We have neither huge fangs nor body armor, like many of the animals out there do. We grew brains and harnessed fire to gain some edge and survive in a pretty harsh environment with drought, predators, and marauding invaders from other tribes. If we made it, we would continue to live.

This definition of the verb *live* essentially means "to continue to exist."

Where? Well, I guess here.

When? It must mean now.

If you're not here, like on this planet, then you are not "living"—at least not here.

And in terms of time, if you're not here right now, then you either existed in the past and are now dead or have not been born yet . . . neither of which would allow you to be here reading this book.

This may all sound trite, but I ask that you humor me. It's the very act of deconstructing what we take for granted that allows for cracks in the concrete—for a glimpse into the deeper realm that we've been trained to look away from. In fact, we're currently living at a time when many of the people stumbling around us are completely unconscious—"Hungry Ghosts" as the Buddhists would call them. They are concerned with the superficial things in life and never stop to think about what this thing called life is really about.

Let's look at the word *life*—another throwaway word that's rooted in the deepest miracle of all.

Here are the top four definitions of *life* from Oxford's online dictionary:

1. The condition that distinguishes animals and
    plants from inorganic matter, including the
    capacity for growth, reproduction, functional
    activity, and continual change preceding death.
    "the origins of life"

2. The existence of an individual human being
    or animal.
    "a disaster that claimed the lives of 266
    Americans"

3. The period between the birth and death of a
    living thing, especially a human being.
    "she has lived all her life in the country"

4. Vitality, vigor, or energy.
    "she was beautiful and full of life"

So life is distinct from inorganic matter.

It grows and reproduces.

It starts and stops, and it has the qualities of vitality,
vigor, and energy.

But let's delve a bit deeper, because somehow the most
miraculous thing we've ever witnessed, the very existence of
life and sentience, is the thing we've all fallen asleep to and
taken for granted.

Sentience?

Here's the definition for *sentient*:

1. Able to perceive or feel things.
    "she had been instructed from birth in the
    equality of all sentient life forms"

Even the dictionary craps out on this definition.

Sentience is the ability to *perceive* that one is alive, aware,
awake, and able to somehow know this. It is the very anchor
of our existence—the hallmark of consciousness.

Who's doing the thinking in your head?

Who's witnessing the thoughts you are perceiving?

Who are we really?

These are the questions posed by the great saints and, frankly, the worthiest ones, in my opinion. These questions lead to ultimate peace, tranquility, and purpose when we shed the artificial constructs of who we're pretending to be so we can relax into the emanation of who we truly are.

LIVING LIFE

To *live life*, then, means we keep the lights on in this process by which inorganic matter somehow gets animated with this thing called "life," which has the qualities of energy, vitality, and vigor. In our case, sentience and consciousness also come with this package. The lights come on, we're *aware* that we exist, we make babies, and then it's over. It starts and stops, and in between we get a chance to pass the torch to the next generation before our time is up.

Done. Lights out. Next.

And what happens in between? What about all the "stuff" we're doing? Is it all meaningless and trite, or is the awareness of being alive, that sentience, actually pointing to something more?

Are we doing something special as we're living life, or are we just *passing time*?

Whether we're doing something awesome or sitting around waiting to die, it seems we're all somehow passing time by living life.

If this thing called life comes with an allocation of "time," then once that's gone, well, then life must be over . . . at least for us.

Let's look at the definition of time.

1. The indefinite continued progress of existence
    and events in the past, present, and future
    regarded as a whole.
    "travel through space and time"
2. A point of time as measured in hours and
    minutes past midnight or noon.
    "the time is 9:30"
3. Time as allotted, available, or used.
    "we need more time"
4. An instance of something happening or being
    done; an occasion.
    "this is the first time I have gotten into debt"

The first definition is the most relevant to our discussion here.

We somehow *exist* here at this moment on planet Earth.

Progress—somehow this existence of ours "moves" or unfolds along this thing we call "time."

Progress of existence . . . a continued yet indefinite *progress of existence* that we measure and plot in this concept called "time," which has a past, present, and future.

It sounds very much to me that time, then, is the very measure of life. It's the measure of our *progress of existence*, and frankly, when that existence ceases to progress, then it ends.

Time is the gift we're given—and the very thing almost everybody complains about.

Time is compressed. It is scarce. It is hurried. There's never enough. And when we have it, we let it "pass" by watching dumb shows and scrolling through social media. We live in troubled times and often reminisce about the good old days. We dream of future times when we'll be healthy, happy, and wealthy. We lament events of the past and look forward to a brighter future that's pain-free and abundant, yet we live like *time paupers* in the present. We're not here. We are unfocused and foggy, stumbling through our days in an endless string of activities that pass the time but don't necessarily gratify us and fill us with vitality, meaning, purpose, or joy.

Just as we suffer in scarcity with time, we also do so with energy and money.

ENERGY

Energy is intimately tied to time. We wake up with it and spend it throughout the day. We need to rest in order to restore it, almost like a pond that fills back up each night. It powers each of our cells and is the *currency* of what keeps the lights on. Without energy, we're dead; we're not even born. It runs the show, and it is needed in every process of our biology.

Energy is the currency of life.

Where does it come from?

The breakdown of molecular bonds in our food. Energy is stored in these bonds, and the process of digestion helps us cleave these molecules and extract the energy inside.

What energy?

Little packets of pure starlight from our sun. Our sun is powering every thought you're having and every itch you scratch.

Plants take the photons of the sun and store them in molecules called carbohydrates. They do this with carbon dioxide from the atmosphere and water. We then eat the plants or eat animals that ate plants and get that energy. A cow spends its day chomping on grass and, with the help of gut bacteria, transforming that grass into energy that's stored in fat and muscle. If we eat the cow, we get energy in many times the concentration of "grass" because the poor cow spent its lifetime eating and converting that sunlight into denser packets of energy that we're now consuming.

This is how life works. Love it or hate it. You can choose to avoid eating the animals (which is a great choice for most), but then you need to make sure you're getting the right balance of calories and nutrients from a variety of vegetables . . . and no, not so many grasses.

Without this energy, we're done. With it, we get up, brush our teeth, and build the Eiffel Tower. We write books, wage wars, ski down mountains, and make babies. All this comes from our local star, the sun.

When the spark of life begins in Mom's uterus, somehow Mom and Dad's genetic material turn on the lights, and the little baby embryo begins to "do things" metabolically, with lots of help from Mom. She eats and sends energy to the baby's cells to replicate like crazy and get the show on the road. Many would argue that life starts at conception . . . *that moment* being the beginning of your *time*.

Therefore, as your time to exist begins, energy becomes the currency of this thing called life.

Where you invest your life's energy will determine what your life will look like.

MONEY

Most people trade their valuable time for money—that's kind of why most people go to work. What's your rate? Per hour, month, or year? There's a monetary value assigned to your time (which goes up with the perceived value of your contribution during that time).

Money is a funny one. It was born from trade and barter and represents a store of value that can be traded for goods and services. In the old days, you'd trade a chicken for a shoe, but then beads and coins came into the picture, which made it easier for people to simply go get what they needed with this "money" instead of walking around looking for someone who had a shoe and also needed a chicken right then.

It allowed trade to become more fluid and efficient and has worked pretty well for several thousand years. It helped us get in and out of the market with the goods we wanted because the medium of exchange created a flow, or a current, among people, hence the word *currency*.

There's a whole can of worms we can get into about fiat currency and the transition of money into credit. Money is now actually fake (because it's not tied to the value of anything real like gold) but still used as a medium of exchange so long as people maintain faith in their currency. It's a deep subject that's beyond the scope of this book, but for our purposes, we need to factor it in because *money buys food, and that's where we get our energy.*

Remember those chemical bonds where energy is stored? Carbohydrates, fats, and proteins lock in the sun's energy. When we consume those plants and animals, we get that energy to sustain life.

Therefore, food sustains life. It keeps us alive, which is kind of important, and we trade time for money and then trade our money for food and shelter. Sure, in the old days (or if you're some survivalist badass), you'd forage, hunt, and farm for your own food. That's a pure transaction with the earth and an important element to understanding reality and our birthright. But putting those ideals aside for now, most of us do some *other* thing for a "job job" in exchange for money and then use that money to buy food from someone else.

Therefore, money is conceptually tied to our survival and must be considered in our calculus here.

OUR "WATER"—THE TRIAD OF TIME, ENERGY, AND MONEY

Time, energy, and money are the three greatest sources of stress, lack, and confusion in our society. All three are intimately linked in a fluid "exchange" that's become a central influence on our lives, even though we tend not to think about it . . . until now.

We're about to embark on a journey in our understanding of time in a way that's very relevant to your life. This isn't some metaphysical exploration of the concept of time that's unanchored in reality. Instead, it's a cold, hard look at how you're existing in time.

How you're living right now is a reflection of the mental, emotional, and spiritual operating system that's driving your *emanation*. How you emanate in this world, in this life, is all a function of personal choice. It's determined by your *focus*.

You determine the "burn rate" of your life.

You ultimately decide where the precious time, money, and energy of your life is allocated.

Think of this blended currency of time, energy, and money as the "Water" of your life force, and think of your life as a garden. You've got "plants," or important things in your life, that you need to keep watering.

The key questions are these:

1. What's currently getting watered and why?
2. Is it enough?
3. What's thriving, and what's withering?
4. What weeds have snuck into your garden?
5. How much time, money, and/or energy does this item need from me to stay alive? How about to thrive?

These are not questions that you need to answer right now. We're going to take a long walk through each of these areas in the chapters of this book, and you'll get a chance to discover your answers yourself. It's personal. The sum total of all the microdecisions you've made, added up with the circumstances, karma, good or bad luck, big wins, and horror stories, has led to the deal you've currently got. It's likely working in some areas and not in others. There will be places you'd like to see improvement.

So let's take a look there—a *real look*. In fact, we're going to *focus* on aspects of your life that may have been neglected for some time.

FOCUS

Focus is a magical thing. It's a superpower that's all but missing in our world today.

In life, when we focus on something important to us, it becomes the *center* of our interest or activity. Focus refers to *clear vision* and implies an *activity* or *action* that brings it about.

We exert energy to attain focus on an object we're looking at or on a topic of interest.

When something is important, we often assume *focus* will naturally happen or be innately there. We do not always think it is something we need to put *effort* into.

This is a big deal because the formula for attaining the life that you choose requires proper use of *focus* and *willpower*.

THE PROBLEM WITH WILLPOWER

If willpower alone did the trick, we wouldn't have a massive industry built around failed New Year's resolutions.

Willpower is the Water in your bucket. You save it up and then empty it all out on a single area of your garden and then wonder why the plants are dying two weeks later.

Look at nature. It's all about sustained nourishment over a longer period of time. Seeds take water and slowly sprout. They wiggle their way to the surface and finally encounter the light of day. Then they fight the harsh elements to remain alive and grow to reproduce and thrive. Sound familiar?

Life has a formula, and the wise follow it and thrive.

When we take the combined power of our attention (or focus) and marry it to our intention (or willpower), we get the clarity and sustained attention we need to grow an idea or important thing in our lives. Think of it like drip irrigation.

In our teens, we'd dump buckets of "Water" everywhere and find more in the tank. It's easy to be sloppy when "youth is wasted on the young." Later in life, perhaps in our thirties, we begin to feel the fatigue setting in. We perhaps shift to a sprinkler system and are a little more careful with our "Water." Most people stop there and get what they get— often with low-grade fatigue and constant frustration.

But I put it to you that there's a better way. Think of tiny little drip irrigation tubes connecting to each hand-picked plant in your Life Garden. You curate what's going to be there, and then, with laser precision, focus just the right amount of Water to keep each plant happy and thriving.

Some plants take more than others, and that's fine. We map it all out and make a life plan that delivers *what life needs* to each. This way, you don't go 40 years watering your career and end up with diabetes and divorce. You don't focus on trinkets you want so much that there's no money for your passions. You don't neglect your health because you think that being a great mom means the ultimate sacrifice of not taking care of yourself, which will eventually mean not being able to care for your kids.

We must find balance and *focus* on sustaining that balance.

The act of focusing is intentional. You have to *exert* some energy to bring something into focus.

So what do we need to do?

We need to develop a practice of focusing on the specific items in our Life Garden every day so that our Water gets delivered as needed.

We are here to *live life* and not pass time blindly. What does that mean?

Let's go back to our definitions.

Living life is the act of staying alive and *existing* while this miracle called life happens and then eventually ends.

Time is the measure of this thing called life. We come in and our time starts. When our time is up, life ceases to exist in us, though it somehow continues on all around us.

Time lives on a continuum with energy and money. Energy is the currency of life itself. Money gets us food and shelter, which provide the energy we need to keep living life.

Time, energy, and money blend together to make a figurative special sauce I'm calling "Water" that we then use and allocate in our personal "Life Garden" to nourish the important items in our life, which we're going to call "plants." In this book, we'll be taking a deep dive into the Life Garden and I'll help you start mapping out your own.

HOW WE GOT HERE

Several years ago, I was a Taoist monk under the surviving abbot of my lineage (Yellow Dragon Monastery in Southern China). I had just learned a new medical Qigong (energy yoga) practice from a visiting master. He taught it in a unique way and said that the only way to "activate" the practice was to do it for 100 days without fail. That would be my *Gong*, or work.

I failed on day 12. I started over.

I failed again on day 46.

I wanted to pretend it hadn't happened. A deal is a deal. I started over.

Each of these first 46 days hurt, and I vowed I'd never falter again. I got to day 100 and completed my first Gong, and then I kept doing them over the years. I have not missed a day (when doing a Gong) since then, and it's been over 25 years.

As I started to "activate" different practices over subsequent Gongs, I started to play with them.

This was in *my own life* as a disciple of a kung fu master and a monk. I was living in the world, going to UCLA, and on my way to becoming a doctor. I had real-world things going on, and I started to introduce goals and other practices into my 100-day Gongs. For example, it would start with a single daily yoga practice, and then I'd add reading, meditation, skipping breakfast, gratitude, cutting gluten, or something else. I've done dozens of these now.

As I did my own thing, the people in my life began to take notice. I was crushing it in different areas of my life. Straight As in school, then a booming practice, hiking the John Muir Trail, *New York Times* best-selling books, movie stuff—it was all working out for me.

I was asked, *Why?*

My answer: "I don't know, but I've been doing this thing."

Then I was asked, *What thing?*

"Well, I split my year into three 100-day sprints with a few weeks in between to think about my life and plan or map out my next Gong."

Often the next question was, *What's a Gong?*

"It's a 100-day commitment to myself. I do daily practices, and I have 30-, 60-, and 100-day goals that I work toward."

And then I would hear, *That sounds interesting. Can you show me how?*

"Sure, I'd be happy to."

It started with me simply mentoring a few friends and family.

That worked.

Then I introduced it to a few select patients:

"Hey, I've been doing this thing, and it's worked for me and a few people. You may want to try it."

One hundred or so days later, pow! Magical transformation in those who did it.

I kept adapting and evolving it over the years and tweaking to see what worked best. Eventually, I expanded it into the concept of the Life Garden, with the categories and instructions that ended up in this book.

The point I'm making is this:

What you're about to read and discover here is the culmination of over 30 years of personal experience and the suggestions, tweaks, and feedback from *thousands* of friends, family, students, and peers who've done Gongs successfully and seen amazing changes in their lives.

This thing has evolved over the years. It is pragmatic and effective and, most importantly, it is not complete. It's been awaiting *you*. Yes, you.

You are here to learn, grow, and *add* to this body of work as your life improves.

HOW TO USE THIS BOOK

Each chapter will break down areas of your life that need to be thought about and mapped out for a future Gong you'll start *after* reading this book. Each chapter will end in an exercise that I ask you to do.

Let me be clear about something. I'm not here to tell you how to live your life, what to do, or even how to do it. That would be arrogant and dismissive of your personal power and role in your own life.

I'm here to humbly share a system or model that has worked for many people. Take it and adapt it to your needs, but know that what's here *works*, so please start with that.

Once you've done a couple of Gongs, you'll get the hang of it and adapt it however best suits you. If it's a win, please share that with my community (theurbanmonk.com) so we can all learn and enjoy the benefits.

In each chapter, we'll lay out a part of the landscape, and then I'll ask that you take the time to write down what's needed for *your* life. Again, this is all about you. It's a personal journey.

YOU decide what's important to you.

YOU allocate YOUR time the way you see fit.

YOU map out your priorities and set the course for YOUR life.

YOU can then make course corrections and adjust where YOUR life is headed.

I'm here to help you make your plan and make suggestions about how to stick to it.

Deal?

Each area or section of your Life Garden is important to take a look at so we can have an overall sense of where you're at. We need to know what's currently drawing all your Water so we can optimize where it goes to better serve you. We'll look at the five areas of Health, Career, Family and Friends, Life's Passions, and Desired Things in your Life Garden. You can map out what's important to you and then see how to adjust things to better serve your priorities.

Let's get into it!

CHAPTER TWO

YOUR LIFE GARDEN

Mastering time starts with understanding where all your time is currently going. What plants are we currently watering with our time, energy, and money?

If your life were to be symbolized by a garden, what would it look like right now? Barren areas on one side and big gnarly weeds on another? What areas would look pretty good, and what others would be neglected?

This honest accounting of where we've been and where we currently stand is an essential step in getting the life we say we want.

We *say* we want certain things in life, yet our actions prove otherwise. What you do on a daily basis is where the rubber hits the road. Your actions speak much louder than words, and when we look at the current state of your Life Garden, we'll see the result of these actions.

Action is energy and focus driven by intent. It will be the catalyst for change that will transform our lives.

But for now, we're stuck with just words.

Where do the words that are not backed by action come in?

Regret.

If you keep saying you want to truly control your blood sugar or write that novel, yet your life reflects a different reality, the steps you've taken have not been aligned with the words you're speaking, so you are lying.

You are lying to yourself, and that hurts.

It starts to wear away at the fabric of your being because your *word* is everything. It's intimately tied to this thing called honor, which is all but gone in our society.

Here's the definition of the verb *honor.*

1. Regard with great respect.
   "they honored their parents in all they did"

2. Fulfill (an obligation) or keep (an agreement).
   "make sure the franchisees honor the terms
   of the contract"

It's the second definition here that's of particular interest. When you "fulfill an obligation" or "keep an agreement," you *honor* it. Therefore, you've acted honorably and have honor.

Our core relationship with the entire Universe is our relationship with ourselves. It's the basis of our identity that's often masked by this thing we call our personality. What we are is not the storefront we present but the underlying essence that lies beneath that.

Our word is tied to that essence.

If we set a priority and say something is important to us, that's a deep and heavy personal proclamation. When we tell ourselves that we're going to do something, write something, avoid something, or what have you, that's an agreement we're making with ourselves.

If we break that deal, we've not kept the agreement and not fulfilled that obligation.

That's a break in our *honor.*

It's a collapse of our *word.*

So many people are doing it all around us that we've come to see this type of behavior is normal.

It isn't.

It's a tear in the fabric of your spiritual life, and it wears away at your honor and integrity.

Integrity implies both moral principles (honor) and structural soundness.

This matters because we're living in a culture where "hungry ghosts" are wandering the streets waiting to be told what to do, how to think, and who to be. They are dishonest with themselves, which makes it easy to be dishonest with each other. It's a spiritual malady that's affecting our culture and infecting our personal psyches.

If we want to restore our personal power and have abundant, amazing lives, we need to snap out of it. This means restoring our honor and integrity *with ourselves.*

The primary interface we have with the world is our deal with ourselves. If we're used to breaking that deal, how are we going to keep our deal with others?

If I'm accustomed to bailing on my resolutions, it's easier for me to be late for a meeting. If I don't do the workouts I promised myself I'd do, then I care less about the report I promised my boss. I may do them because I'd get fired otherwise, but in the end, the fabric of my word has been compromised.

Until now.

Enough of this nonsense. What we're about to do is right a wrong that's challenged humans since the beginning of time.

One translation of the word *genesis* is *"As I speak, I create."*

What reality are you spinning out with your words? Are you backing them with action and integrity to make them a reality, or are your words empty?

Think about that next time you talk some stupid nonsense that you know you'll never back up. You're spinning chaos into the Universe and chipping away at your own integrity and honor. This is the root of a spiritual malady that's been plaguing us for millennia.

We're here to fix that. Starting today.

Right now, in fact.

It's time to start gardening your life in a way that honors your dreams, backs your words, and gets you to think twice before saying things you don't have the capacity to manifest yet.

YOUR CURRENT SITUATION

The first step in fixing a problem is identifying the issues. You may think you need more time, but you have the same amount of time as any other person each day.

Where's yours going?

As we go through this chapter, we're going to partition the Life Garden into various areas that help us think about our life and our priorities. Your task is going to be to look at each area and be radically honest with yourself about how well you're doing there. It's always a work in progress, and there's never going to be perfect balance in all areas of your Garden. Life isn't that neat. At times, Career will be heavy. At others, a baby is born, and you're not sleeping much. All your time gets sucked down a channel for many months, and you don't have much choice—you must live those hours and find balance somehow. Things move and change, and priorities shift—that's normal. Time gets reallocated regularly.

Your current situation is just a snapshot in time, but it's likely also a reflection of the patterns of thought, beliefs, habits, and blind spots that have led you to trudge through life without questioning much.

Now we question everything.

When you're navigating in the backcountry, your map may show you crossing a river at a certain place, yet when you get there, the bridge is washed out. That's life. You may need to hike upstream a couple miles and cross there. Keep your eyes on the prize. Keep going and adjust. It's always important to get your bearings and know where you stand. Your life depends on it when you're out in the wild. That's a critical first step because you can't get to your destination if you can't *plot your starting point.* As you continue, you make adjustments, which is completely natural.

So we're going to do that now.

We'll look at what your life looks like right now and factor that into your journey as we then plot a course toward where you want to go.

Here's the challenge.

Most of us talk about wanting to summit great mountains but won't admit that we're standing waist-deep in a bog several valleys away. We may need to trudge a few hundred miles before we're in the clear. That's fine. If that's where you currently stand, let's be honest about it so we can make a plan and get you out. I promise there's hope for you.

Every thousand-mile journey begins with the first step, but that doesn't mean just start walking. You've tried that before. In fact, life may feel like a long, painful march that never gets you anywhere. So let's stop marching for a second. In which direction is our thousand-mile journey? Where do we want to go, and where are we starting from?

Let's examine the five areas of the Life Garden now. This is going to be your homecoming as you take stock of where you currently stand so you can decide where you want to go and then map out a course that'll get you there.

THE AREAS OF YOUR LIFE GARDEN

Over the years, I've landed on five broad areas I've worked on in my own Life Garden. These categories have pretty much worked for the thousands of people who have done this. That said, they aren't set in stone. If you want to focus on other areas in your life, make another category or cut out one of mine.

The point is this: we need to account for your whole life—the entirety of your being—in this landscape. We can't allocate a budget to water a handful of areas in your life and then find out you've got another category that's draining time, energy, and money "off the books."

That's cheating yourself.

You don't need to show this to anybody, so please don't be dishonest with yourself—that's an integrity thing. In fact, the weird dark alleys you don't want to look down are likely the places where a good amount of your power is trapped. *Look there.*

As we walk through this symbolic Life Garden framework, I'll give examples of things that should fall under each category. Just take note and humor me for now. Again, this has worked for many people before you, and over the years, I've learned that we're not all that different when it comes to the broad categories, even if we think we are. Later, you can adjust, modify, and make improvements for yourself.

Area #1—Health

I'm starting with health because, without it, the show is over. In fact, our health and our time are intimately interwoven and interconnected in a profound way.

When our health meter is at zero, our time is up.

It's kind of that simple. We need to sustain our health in order to buy more time on this planet. The very life force that we spoke about in the first chapter is measured in this thing called health. Our *Vitality* is the abundance or overflow of this energy of life. It's the energy that handles our body's day-to-day needs and then overflows into higher brain function, a sense of humor, moral behavior, and spontaneous running, jumping, skipping, and laughing.

It's the energy that makes us feel "alive."

Does this seem like a distant fantasy?

If so, you're not alone.

We live in a culture that's been chipping away at our Vitality for years. We feel diminished and depleted. We are robbing Peter to pay Paul and are scraping energy from coffee and sugar just to get through our days.

Is it any wonder we don't have enough energy to fuel our dreams, call an old friend, or build a new shed in the backyard?

If you lack the energy to fuel your day-to-day metabolic needs, you certainly don't have what it takes to invest more energy into a future you'd like to see. You're living on the energetic bread line and are struggling to simply get by.

Let's set the table here and be very clear about something:

Your health and your energy are inextricably tied.

So how do we start looking at our health?

It starts with an assessment of how we're doing right now.

Do you have good energy levels that are sustained throughout the day?

If not, when do you dip, or is it not there upon waking?

Do you have medical conditions that you've been dealing with for some time?

Are they under control?

Are you doing everything your doctors told you to do to manage your condition, or are other priorities crowding this out?

Are there lifestyle measures you can take, beyond pills, to improve your condition?

Are you sleeping enough?

Are you resting when tired?

Are you getting daily exercise?

What's your diet like?

There's about 10,000 books on each of the areas I mentioned here, so let's go big picture and help you understand how to look at all of this.

Good health is not an option.

It is a necessity if you want to live a rich, meaningful life with accomplishments you can be proud of. Energy is the gas your vehicle of a body needs to run. You can't plan a road trip with an empty tank, a busted transmission, and bald tires.

We need to fix your health in order to get you on the road.

If you have orthopedic concerns, there are doctors for that. There are physical therapists, acupuncturists, chiropractors, massage therapists, and a whole host of other allied health professionals who can help. Seek them out.

If these services are unaffordable, then get online and search for exercises that can help. There are books and resources online to help you manage almost any condition. The information is there. Understand the value of your health enough to prioritize it.

My first film, *Vitality*, broke health into four general categories that need to be in balance: Diet, Exercise, Sleep, and Mindset. Let's look at each because, together, they make up overall health and Vitality.

Diet

Your diet is a critical part of your health, as we now know most inflammation starts in the gut.

Cleaning up your diet is the highest-impact action you can do for good health. It's also the cheapest. After all, you buy food and eat daily. You buy groceries each week and can make changes at the grocery store that will fundamentally transform your health and therefore your life. Broccoli is cheap. Most vegetables are. High-sugar and processed foods are also cheap but will eventually kill you. You're the one buying what's in the cart. You are the one putting the items in there. What vegetables and other healthy foods can you put in there? The choice to be healthy starts there.

What if food were your medicine instead of the hundreds of dollars' worth of supplements you think you need? What if you improved your health by simply choosing to eat healthy foods?

Whether it's to fight and reverse diabetes, heart disease, allergies, or a bum shoulder, diet is the key to your health, and changing it will unlock vast reserves of wasted, trapped, and unconverted energy (stored as fat) in your body.

This book can't do a deep dive into all things diet, or it'll be 500 pages, so let me make it simple: eat lots of vegetables, and when you think it's enough, eat more.

Our microbiome is a vast ecosystem of bacteria and other microscopic organisms that thrive on fiber and plant polyphenols. We've co-evolved with these bugs. We feed them, and they produce B vitamins, hormones, energy, immune function, and much more for us. They want fibrous plants instead of starch and processed sugar.

Go back.

Go heavy on clean produce that's free of pesticides. Eat at least two types of veggies that are different colors with each meal. Eat fermented foods daily (ideally with each meal), and if you eat meat, get it from a clean source that's trusted and safe. If an animal was fed toxic food all its life, the toxicity is now concentrated in its tissue, and you're eating it. Toxicity bioaccumulates and prevents our mitochondria from producing energy effectively.

As our ability to produce energy diminishes, we have less to go around, and we feel tired, sick, and bogged down. With less energy, we don't feel like exercising and doing the right thing. It's a downward spiral that robs us of our dreams and aspirations by slowly taking away our health.

It all goes back to eating right.

These are the basics, but in my experience, 95 percent of patients are not following this advice and are trying the latest shortcut cute thing that won't work either. Start here and then, yes, there are specific strategies around fasting, carb loading, keto, and a million other things that can get you the rest of the way there.

If you have food allergies, figure out the workarounds. If you can't handle that much fiber yet, start slowly and ramp up. If dairy bothers you by giving you gas and brain fog, stop eating it. Your body thinks it's poison, and it should be avoided. The same could be said for gluten, shellfish, peanuts, or soy.

Find out what your body is *telling you* it doesn't like, and stop eating it.

Follow this basic dietary advice, and you'll be more than halfway there.

Exercise

Still water breeds poisons. Similarly, a stagnant human gets creaky and tired.

We need to move daily, and if that's not part of your routine, I strongly urge you to add it immediately. Your life won't move if you aren't moving. As you start fixing your diet and stop taking in foods that inflame your gut and set off your immune system, you will unlock more energy from your food and start to feel more energized, which will help you feel like moving again.

Exercise is the number one way to keep your heart healthy (which means more time on the planet) and your brain healthy (which means having the focus and clarity to manifest the life you choose).

Movement is not an option; it's a mandatory requirement of a healthy life.

As you look at your current situation, be honest about how much exercise you're getting. We'll be doing a lot of work mapping out some better balance in your life, but I can't emphasize enough that daily movement needs to be in there. Without it, our light flickers and we don't have the power to plan and stick to our goals, let alone face life's many challenges.

Sleep

Another nonnegotiable area in health is sleep. We can't live without it, yet it's the first thing to go when times get crunchy and we get busy. It's also the thing we tend to lose when our minds are troubled over some drama or money shortfall.

Here's why it's important: sleep is how we restore our energy for the next day, repair tissue, detoxify the brain, cycle hormones, work out the day's issues, and do a gazillion other things.

What goes up must come down, and over millennia, our species has gotten less sleep at night. Nighttime is when predators are out. They have about five to nine times better night vision than humans, so we didn't stand a chance. Frankly, the only thing that saved us was our ability to harness fire.

In the Kabbalah, it is said that man was given a divine gift that none of the other animals had—the gift and responsibility of harnessing fire.

We used fire to light the night sky and keep warm. We'd huddle around it and tell stories and make music, the basis of our social structure and need to connect. Predators were terrified of it and left us alone to build community, sing songs, perform rituals, and tell stories.

This brings us to an important consideration about sleep.

It has changed with the modern world.

That fire we'd huddle around emitted a red-shifted light. Today, most of our screens emit blue-shifted light, which tells our brains (the pineal gland, to be specific) to stay awake and keep foraging for food. This prevents the release of melatonin and keeps us awake in bed.

Nighttime used to be cold, and our bodies adapted to sleep better as we huddled up to keep warm.

It was relatively quiet. The sounds of crickets and grasses dancing in the wind, or perhaps a babbling brook or stream in the background, helped lull us to sleep. That was it. The entry of a predator meant a real emergency was at hand, but that was occasional, not frequent.

Today, sirens and screeching car tires alert us to trouble, although it rarely applies to us. The artificial sounds around us can stimulate our brains and keep us awake.

We used to go down with music and make love before drifting off into oblivion. Today we take our worries and bills into the bed with us, again compromising our deep sleep.

All of this leads to poor recovery cycles, which eventually hurt our health.

Simply put, we can't be healthy without sleep. Many have tried to cheat it, and I've seen every hack out there come and go. It's all cute, but nothing replaces sleep.

As you look at mapping out your Life Garden, don't cheat sleep. In fact, most people find that factoring more of it into their lives tends to help all the other categories.

Mindset

Stress is killing us and causing all sorts of health problems in our society. I mention this here because of its noxious tie-in with health. You simply *must* have some form of stress management built into your days in this world.

Stress elevates cortisol levels, which impact our sleep and energy metabolism. It causes us to store fat because the body thinks there's a crisis and it needs to conserve energy.

It's a bad deal.

Stress used to be a lion chasing you or a neighboring village attacking. It meant life or death, and it triggered a very specific reaction in the body that helped us fight or flee to save our lives. Afterward, we'd shake it off and recover so life could go back to normal.

Today, it's death by a thousand cuts. Every siren, surprise bill, bad phone call, or headline in the news can trigger the same response. Our ancient biological systems have not evolved as fast as our technological world. We are not adapting fast enough to offset all the triggers that flip us out.

The result?

Well, look around you. We're a mess and don't see a way out.

Enter meditation.

You can't think clearly if the walls are caving in, and frankly, they always are nowadays. You need a routine that'll help offset this energy in the modern world in order to stay healthy. Meditation solves this problem. Consider meditation as mental flossing. It's just good hygiene to meditate, pray, or do yoga, Qigong, or something else to help offset your stress in the modern world.

Vitality

We've mentioned *Vitality* a few times already. It'll keep coming up. To me, Vitality is the summation of all our health areas all working together in harmony and balance. You can't eat right and exercise like a beast yet not sleep a wink at night. You can't meditate all day yet eat like a pig—your heart will stop.

Diet, exercise, sleep, and mindset need to work together so health can flourish.

When you're healthy, your body feels light, energized, and filled with Vitality. You feel well and can make good decisions that come from the higher parts of the brain that allow for moral reasoning, the negation of impulses, and critical thinking. The energy that comes from your food goes to the right places and powers up a healthy brain that helps you make good decisions and stick to your plans. You have enthusiasm in life and optimism for the future.

All of this will continue to come into play as we map out our Life Gardens.

Assessing Your Health

Assessing your current health state is the place to start.

I've included a link to a basic Medical Symptom Questionnaire (MSQ) in the back of this chapter for you. It was developed by the Institute for Functional Medicine and is a great tool to see where you're at.

The first step in plotting a course for your health is taking a cold, hard look at where you stand. Do the assessment, or better yet, find a good doctor who can help you navigate any health concerns.

Health is the flower that only blooms when the root is in good shape. The root of the human body is the gut. According to the ancients, all disease starts there. Heal your gut, fix your diet, move around, get good sunlight, and drink plenty of water. We've heard all of this before.

Now is the time to actually do something about it.

We'll make a plan in later chapters, but the first stop, again, is being honest about where we stand.

Do the MSQ right now, before moving to the next section.

You need you to be healthy.

Area #2—Career

The Career section of the Garden is usually the one that pulls all the Water for many of my patients. People tend to emphasize their work because they owe tons of money from school, have to pay off a car, and have to provide food and shelter for themselves and/or their families. They're pulled into a financial vacuum that demands more and more money each year, calling on them to step up and work themselves to the bone.

People get diabetes and heart attacks. People die from stress and overwork. They get divorces and lose friends.

That's obviously on the bad side.

People also get Nobel prizes, find cures for diseases, and have very fulfilling lives because of their careers. Your work can be incredibly rewarding and satisfying.

All things in balance.

We're here to make work a win for you and have it live in harmony with other areas of your life. That's not easy in a culture where many people define themselves by what they do.

Our very identity is tied up in what we do, and that's the hallmark of our sick culture. It's a spiritual ailment to mix up who we truly are with how we pass our time. Now, your career and your identity may be in harmony, and that's great, but we're going to make sure that's the case and give you some time to examine that.

For most of us, we've got to work, produce, create, clock in, or do whatever we do to get this thing called money that pays for our food, shelter, and lifestyle.

So how's this section of the Life Garden doing for you?

Are you hating your job and sucking it up each day to go in for work? Are you annoyed that it's only Tuesday and always looking forward to the weekend? Is "TGIF" your favorite saying? If so, then we've got some thinking to do here. Hating what you do eight hours a day adds up to a sucky lifetime that's full of bitterness, regrets, and probably some Prozac.

Going to a "job job" that you hate is a surefire way of letting one area of your Life Garden suck all the Water away from your life.

We will fix it.

First, we need to examine it.

If you love your job or career, that's great news. You're in a smaller club, but you're also possibly guilty of overworking and crowding out other areas of your life. Are your kids paying the price for your passion for work? How many big life events have you missed? How's your marriage or your physical and mental health?

There is no right or wrong answer here—only the one that is true to you. We each need to find our own balance between all the areas of our lives, and right now, we're looking at Career.

Are you happy and fulfilled with your work?

Are you miserable in your job?

Is your career depleting another area of your life? Which one(s)?

Do you have a plan for where you want your career to go?

Have you mapped out retirement and what that would look like?

Are you terrified that you won't be able to retire?

Do you never want to retire because you love what you do?

All of these are things to consider as you assess your current state of affairs in this category. There's nothing to do here (yet) except think about all the areas of your life that are being touched by your career and decide whether or not you feel you have balance there.

We all need help here. Work can take over, and when there's money stress, it's hard to be a good spouse, parent, or even driver on the road.

Work spills over into all areas of life because it's the abstract connection to our very survival. Being late on a bill impacts your credit, which reduces your ability to function in a credit-based economy. Worse, you can have your power shut off, be evicted, have your car taken, and have your accounts seized. If that's all tied to survival, which it is, then your amygdala is stuck in "fight or flight," and that stress doesn't just feel real; *it is real.*

Stress releases cortisol, which makes you store fat and restricts your access to efficient energy pathways in your body. It impacts your sleep and mood.

That said, I'm not some idealistic hippie telling you to quit your job. You need to make money, keep the lights on, and feed your family. I don't make the rules, and I live in the same economy you do. We need to find a way for you to do so without crushing your health or estranging your children.

Let's take an assessment of where you stand in your Career area currently, and be honest. From there, I'd like to suggest that you think about ways to improve your efficiency in this area so you can trade less time for money and make tons more money.

Do you worry about money on a daily or weekly basis?

Are you constantly holding bills until there's enough to pay them?

Are you afraid to upset a boss that's rude to you because you can't afford to get fired?

Are your credit cards always on the full side?

Do you go into overdraft in your bank account more than once a quarter?

Are you happy with your retirement plan?

Does it stress you out to even think about retirement?

Does the thought of money make you cringe?

Do an honest accounting of where the Water in this area of your Garden is going right now so we can make a plan and stick to it.

Area #3—Family and Friends

We live in a very *independent* culture that was spawned from tribal roots that were very *interdependent*. In the old days, your tribe was your extended family, and you had each other's backs. From hunting and foraging to waging war and forming neighborhoods, we stuck together and looked after one another. Nobody was left alone; each was part of a whole.

That's an awesome, comforting feeling to have, but it's also sometimes unnerving if you ask people who still live in such cultures. There's *zero* privacy, and everyone is up in your business. People sit around and gossip about others and tell you what you should be doing with your life. Yuck.

So where does that leave us?

For many people, that leaves us in some funky middle ground where we don't hang with our extended families that often and we've selected our group of friends. We cowboys and cowgirls rode off into the sunset and left the old world behind. We have a culture that was formed on ideas of fierce independence—leaving the old world, protesting the Catholic Church, and doing it a new way, a *better* way.

We tolerate our parents or our in-laws for a couple of days during the holidays and bemoan the awkward dinners. Some of us have our drinking buddies, college friends, or sports club peeps, and we make the plans we want to make. Others have lost contact with the high school group, and our work "friends" kind of suck. We've shrunken our social circles to a few people here and there that we catch a movie with. Or perhaps it's even more isolated. We hang with Brent4165 in an online shooter game and chitchat while we tuck out of reality altogether.

We may have lost the baby with the bathwater.

There's a bit of a loss (a tragic one) of something we've been hardwired to do for millennia—*connect with other people.*

This isn't just warm fuzzy stuff. Plenty of studies show that isolation can lead to depression and suicide. It can also lead to further alienation and absurd things like school shootings with assault rifles.

We no longer understand each other, so we further isolate and entrench ourselves.

We're losing our empathy.

We need people in our lives.

We need love.

We need to be heard.

We need connection.

This is causing a major existential dilemma on the planet.

In this section, I want you to think about your current state of affairs when it comes to family and friends.

Where do you stand with your parents, if they're alive?

Where do you stand with your spouse, partner, or lover?

Are you alone and lonely?

Where do you stand with your kids?

Your oldest friends?

Your colleagues?

Your new friends from the last few years?

Your exes?

Your pets?

Just think about all the beings in your life, and do an assessment of how much time and energy you're putting into them. How much Water is going to this part of the Garden? Are you happy with the outcome?

When my kids were born, I disappeared into Diaper and Insomnia Land for a couple of years. Some of my single buddies didn't understand this and were irritated with me. I understood their frustration, but I was watering other areas of the Garden. As soon as I could, I reached out and dripped more Water onto those friendships and revived years of camaraderie, but it didn't come without drama.

Others I've let go of. Those were the harder decisions. There were a couple of guys whose lives were stuck, and they spewed bitterness every time we hung out. They never took advice from anybody and loved to complain. I have no time for that. You have to identify how much Water you have to allocate in each area and make some difficult decisions.

Pull the weed.

Do you have these people in your life?

Are they your parents?

Ouch.

We've got lots of co-dependent relationships that come from the interdependent world of family and tribe. Some may need to be cut, and it sucks. That's on you to figure out. They're your personal relationships, and it's your personal math once you have a good sense of what else you need to water in your Life Garden.

It may mean better boundaries. It may mean a good-bye note. It's your call.

If you're in an abusive relationship, you need to get out. It never gets better, and you're spending more time making excuses for your abuser than you should. Cut and run as best you can. If there are kids involved, get the courts involved. There are domestic violence hotlines and people in every town waiting to help you. Don't tolerate abuse . . . ever.

Friends and family can nurture our souls, warm our hearts, and bring joy to our days when they are in our lives in balance. If you are swamped with social obligations and can't figure out when you're going to do that project you need to do, then you've got some work to do. Make solid boundaries around your time, and allocate what you can for your friends.

It'll be hard. But at this stage, I'm simply asking that you assess where you're at in each of these categories and jot some thoughts down. Later, as we circle in on making a plan for you, some tough decisions may need to be made, but you can't do any of it until you've laid it all out in front of yourself.

We're going to continue our journey into the various areas of your Life Garden. Once we've taken a good look and surveyed the land, we'll have a better idea. You may find some healthy-looking weeds you may not have seen until now. You've been unconsciously watering them for so long that they look like healthy plants. Once we've had a look, you can decide what's truly important to you and *water that*.

Area #4—Life's Passions

We all have dreams and aspirations. At least we used to have some.

What happened to them, and where are they now?

A kid wants to be an astronaut.

Someone dreams of painting in Paris.

Seeing the pyramids and exploring ancient tombs may be your deal.

This area is often where we pick up the most hurt, vitriol, bitterness, embarrassment, dismay, or whatever other emotion comes with unfulfilled dreams.

Somehow, life got in the way, and now you're stuck in some "job job" with kids who won't listen to you, a sick mom, a dying cat, and bills up to your ears. Even if you could afford a trip to Paris, your damned hip won't let you walk around anymore, and so on.

This loss of dreams is very common and the cause of millions of bad attitudes, asshole personalities, and alcohol addictions.

You had dreams. You had plans. Now you're bitter.

Your current life is the summation of all your good and bad choices and all the circumstances that came your way. Some you handled the best you could, and others—well, those you probably could have made better choices.

That's life.

We've all got regrets.

I've made plenty of mistakes in my day. I still pick myself up and decide what the next right move is to be afterward and so will you.

I want you to think about all the dreams and passions you have and/or had. Not all is lost.

Once we map out what's important to you, it's critical that you water this area of your Life Garden so you can finally tap into your passions.

Life is to be lived and enjoyed. It needs fulfillment and adventure, or else we don't feel alive.

News flash: You are going to die.

Your time here will end, and you have a choice. Do you want it to end with or without the experience of the passion you have longed for?

It's time to grab the bull by the horns and start living life.

It may take a few years to fulfill your passion if it's a big bite, and that's fine. The time to start watering that part of your Garden is now. Even a few drops each day or week will help bring life to your dreams and move you closer to making them a reality. It's a must.

For now, just go back and start jotting down what your passions are. What's on your bucket list—the things you must see, do, or accomplish before you die? Even if it sounds unattainable or unrealistic, write it all down.

Do you want to travel? Where?

Are you fighting for a cause?

Have you been meaning to learn how to dance?

Have you been stalling out on joining a club or group?

Don't sell yourself short. The time to manage your expectations will come when all the plants you need to water have been identified. Then, we'll make a plan and allocate Water as your life's priorities require it. You can't lose the house over a trip, but you might be able to cut your cable service and work a side hustle to make it happen.

We can map out a long-term year plan for some of this if need be. Let's map it out first, and then you can decide.

Get to writing!

Area #5—Desired Things

Toys are not all that bad. In fact, they're the bounty life has to offer in our short visit here on planet Earth. This area of the Garden will honor what it is you want materially in your life.

Do you want land in Montana? A boat? A diamond necklace? A helicopter?

I don't know and don't care, so long as it doesn't harm others or the planet. We've come to a time in our collective history when we can no longer burn it down at the expense of the ecosystem.

In my humble opinion, material things are inherently fine so long as they are clean and are produced ethically.

So what is it that you want in life?

Don't be shy. Jot down the things that you've always wanted to acquire, the things that you think will make you happy.

There's nothing wrong with wanting these things and buying them, so long as they don't upset the balance of your Garden.

For example, you may be on a fixed salary but really want a BMW so you can feel rich and show the folks you grew up with that you've made something of yourself. That's okay, I guess, unless you go sign a bad lease deal with 30 percent interest that puts you into payments that stress you out each month.

Now you're working overtime, neglecting your kids, and losing sleep over a dumb car that drives slightly better than the Honda you traded in. You're not enjoying the drive, though, because you've got your mind on your bills.

That's an issue. You're pulling Water away from vital areas of your Garden to pay for a thing that's too heavy. In this case, I'd say probably no BMW for now.

The flip side would be if you grew up with parents who had survived the Depression and were forced to be frugal. Now you're sitting on multiple six figures in equity but still buy your shoes from the bargain store.

Go get some Nikes and enjoy your life. Buy some for a kid in need if you can't get over your upbringing. Loosen up and enjoy your money.

The point I'm making is that the balance of your Life Garden will be different. It varies in every case.

Make a list of what things you really want, and think about the list. Are these things you really want, or have you been trained or convinced to think or say you want them?

Some kids say they want Ferraris. Have you sat in one? They're super uncomfortable to sit in for a long time.

Other kids want ponies, but precious few would pick up the poop.

Now that you're an adult, what is it? A Birkin bag? An F-150 truck? A private jet?

That's expensive and wasteful.

I'm not saying don't get the things you want. I'm simply saying think about it. Are you really that busy, or are you trying to look cool, fit in, and belong?

Jot down what you want, and then think about if it'll really make you happy. If so, then keep it on the list, and we'll find a way to water it.

COMING TO GRIPS

Radical honesty about where you currently stand is difficult. It can be downright miserable. After all, we live in a culture that's mired in conspicuous consumption. Image is everything. I personally know dozens of health celebrities and gurus who schedule photo shoots for their Instagram feeds.

Makeup, wardrobe, lighting, and thousands of shots taken to pull the dozen or so pictures that make up their feed.

It's all fake.

That's not their real life. It's the one they want you to see, the "storefront" image that makes you believe certain things about them.

They may be saying, "Take my protein shake and look like me," but what's missing from that message is the decade of testosterone creams, face-lifts, cold sculpting, and stimulants they're taking "on the side," not to mention the last-minute water fasting, makeup, and Photoshop touch-ups.

So if the gurus can't be real, how can you?

Simple. Drop the bullshit and come to grips with reality. It's the only way to heal.

Are you doing well financially or two months away from bankruptcy?

Are you sleeping well, or is the Ambien, wine, pot, and Benadryl cocktail doing the job for you?

Are you being the best parent you can be?

Best spouse?

Most dedicated employee?

Let's be honest. Please.

The only way your life is going to change for the better is if you start this journey on solid ground.

Look at each area of your Life Garden (Health, Career, Family and Friends, Life's Passions, and Desired Things), and do an honest assessment of what's needed for each to thrive. Fill out the columns at the end of this chapter and take a day or so to make sure you don't miss anything, which we all do. We all instinctively look away.

From there, look at the relative balance between the areas. Say 45 percent of your "Water" is going to Career, then 15 percent to Family and Friends, and so forth. Estimate what percentage of your total "Water" is going where in your *current* Life Garden.

This is a very important point.

Do not map out your aspirations on this Current Status page. We tend to pace, projecting our *desired reality* onto our current one and are often not honest with ourselves about what's actually going on. Don't do that. We will spend the rest of this book working to map out a brighter, more balanced future with Water going to all the right areas for you, but this first step is critical.

Be honest. Where are you at right now, without deception and projection?

It may feel glum right now. That's fine.

If this seems downright depressing, and you're feeling like you don't want to do this or look at your life, you're in exactly the right place.

The Buddha spoke of human suffering coming from aversions and cravings. We want to feel good and happy and move away from discomfort and sadness.

Perhaps you've moved away from reality for years because it's not gone as well as you'd hoped. Thinking about the past could be depressing. The present might not look much better, so you live in anticipation of a better future.

We live in a culture that thrives on telling you what you want to hear because it sounds easy.

Get six-pack abs in four minutes.

Look 40 years younger with this miracle cream.

Feel like a teenager again by drinking this can of soda.

Do you want a better life?

Then *let's get real.*

This brings us back to that concept of time. My Zen master always used to say, "If you want to see what your future looks like, look at the last 10 years, and know that it'll look the same unless you step into the present moment and change yourself."

This requires radical honesty and dealing with a little discomfort.

If you want to change your stars, you need to come home to the present moment and do an honest accounting of your current state of affairs. Then we begin our journey. Remember the navigation example. You can't set your course if you don't have your bearings. That's what we're doing right now.

MANAGING EXPECTATIONS

Rome wasn't built in a day, although it was burned down in a day by the Visigoths. From the ashes rose something new, and it took centuries to get to the "height" of the Roman Empire. It also involved mass genocide, rape, pillaging, slavery, brutal war crimes, corruption, scandal, and all sorts of other atrocities that somehow became glorified as the birth of Western civilization. How about we carve out a better example in our day?

Pardon the digression . . .

My point here is that change takes time.

You may look at your current situation and find yourself in the bog longing for a mountain peak. You're much more likely in that scenario to fall for a "get rich quick" type scheme, where you're told you can skip all the work and end up with some magical, heavenly outcome.

Sorry, it doesn't work that way. You've already tried that out, and you're here now. *Doing the work* might sound awful, but it isn't. It's the only game in town to actually heal your life. For real.

This requires managing expectations. If you've spent 55 years getting yourself into the "mess" you're currently in, it may take several months, if not a few years, to work your way forward into a better situation. Will it all suck? No.

You'll gradually feel better and have more energy, clarity, focus, and enthusiasm along the way, but it won't feel like angels singing and glorious bells ringing from day one.

Let's roll up our sleeves and get to work, knowing it may take a little while to get to our long-term goals. This is the beginning of a process that will become a new operating system. You will constantly be working toward balance in life, and you will get better at it every day. It will become a game that you improve at and start to win. Not every day, but the wins will start to stack up until you become an all-star.

Sound good?

Great. Fill out the tables at the end of the chapter, and spend some time being honest with yourself. Remember, you don't need to share this with anyone. It's your book, so guard it closely, and allow yourself to be honest in all areas.

LIFE GARDENING HOMEWORK

In each area of your Life Garden, we're going to do an overall assessment of where you currently stand, rating you between 1 and 10, with 1 being the lowest and 10 being amazing. Give a number to each area, and then do the corresponding exercise.

THE FIVE AREAS OF MY LIFE GARDEN

Health

My Current Status in Health

0   1   2   3   4   5   6   7   8   9   10

Please go to theurbanmonk.com/focus to get your overall Vitality Score.

The survey you find there will tally your score in each category and average them all for a "Vitality Score" you can work from. It's a great starting point.

Once you have your score, we're going to have you reassess it now and again to track your progress. Just store it in a safe place so we can come back to it in the coming weeks to track your improvement.

Here's a link to the Medical Symptom Questionnaire from the Institute for Functional Medicine: theurbanmonk.com/focus.

Again, fill out the survey and the MSQ, and you'll have a good idea of where to start in the Health area of your Garden. These quizzes and assessments are a reflection of your health state *right now* and not how you'd like to feel.

Career

My Current Status with Career

0   1   2   3   4   5   6   7   8   9   10

What's the current status of your career? Fill out the following questions, and keep digging if there's more. Really get into it, and make sure you're honest about where you currently stand.

> Are you happy and fulfilled with your work?
> Are you miserable in your job?
> Is your career depleting another area of your life? Which one(s)?
> Do you have a plan for where you want your career to go?
> Have you mapped out retirement and what that would look like?

Are you terrified that you won't be able to retire?

Do you never want to retire because you love what you do?

I've also compiled some great financial assessment tools for you. Please go to theurbanmonk.com/focus to get access to them. If money is what's sucking your energy dry, it's really important to take a cold, hard look at it. Please do this now.

Family and Friends

My Current Status with Family and Friends

0   1   2   3   4   5   6   7   8   9   10

Here are some general questions for you to answer for yourself. Answer all that apply to you, and if there's more you'd like to record at this stage in the work, please do so here so you can come back and reference it later.

Where do you stand with your parents, if they're alive?

Where do you stand with your spouse, partner, or lover?

Your siblings?

Aunts and uncles?

Cousins?

Are you alone and lonely?

Are you surrounded by toxic people?

Where do you stand with your kids?

Your oldest friends?

Your colleagues?

Your new friends from the last few years?

Your exes?

Your pets?

Think about all the people in your life, and do an assessment of how much time and energy you're putting into them. How much water is going to this part of the Garden? Are you happy with the outcome? Spend some time thinking about it as you fill in this section.

Passions

My Current Status with Passions

0   1   2   3   4   5   6   7   8   9   10

We're going to map this out in much further detail in Chapter 7. Right now, list what the current passions are that you're actually spending time on. I understand that this may be a starving area, but it's important to understand what you're working with.

What have you accomplished that you're happy about?

What are you getting to do that nourishes your soul?

Where are you doing things that simply make you happy and fill your tank?

What currently sparks the most joy for you in life?

Desires

My Current Status with Desires

0   1   2   3   4   5   6   7   8   9   10

Where are you currently at with the things you've wanted in life? It's okay to want things in life, and you can find a healthy balance between material objects and life experiences.

What's the current state of the things you've got?

Your car?
House?
Toys?
Jewelry?
Clothing?

What have you bought for yourself that you're happy about and proud of?

Again, list anything else that comes to mind right here so you have a good log of where you started. These are not things you *want* but things you currently have.

CHAPTER THREE

THE MAGICAL FORMULA FOR TIME MASTERY

There's been a lot of talk about the power of intention. In my opinion, this talk only addresses half of the matter. In fact, I believe it reinforces the fruitless efforts of countless millions of people into failed resolutions, especially over New Year's Day.

Willpower has become a self-help buzzword, but willpower can be ineffective for people if it's completely unfocused—or if *you are* completely unfocused.

Think about a drunk boxer throwing wide, swinging punches in the ring, hoping to get a lucky knockout, in opposition to a sober, serious, tactical fighter who remains calm, collected, and patient, looking for openings in their opponent's defenses. The tactical fighter understands that 12 rounds is a long time and paces themselves while seeking opportunities and conserving energy, all with their eye on the prize. This is the fighter I have my money on.

That's how you're going to learn to look at life.

If you want to fulfill your destiny, you need to look at the long game and stay under your breath. Panting and throwing haymakers are desperation plays. They seldom win the match, but they are how most people try to attain their dreams and aspirations, only to deflate completely when they fail to work . . . *again.*

This has everything to do with intention.

Intention is backed by your energy. It's a bucket of Water that you've saved up drop by drop, until you've mustered up enough Water to make one big push.

Then another precious year of your life goes by, and you have some regrets.

Perhaps you didn't exercise much this year . . . again.

Perhaps the holidays got the best of you and you overate.

Maybe you slacked off on the project you said you'd launch last year.

Or maybe you had a terrible year in sales at work.

Someone may have died, or a divorce might have finally gone through.

Whatever it is, that's it—another year down, and less to show for it than you'd have liked.

You're annoyed and *promise yourself* you'll do better. Next year is a new year, and you're going to turn over a new leaf!

So starting January 2 (you need a day to recover from your hangover), you're going to go to the gym daily, eat only healthy food, build an Eiffel Tower in your backyard, and make $2 million *this year.*

And then what happens?

Inertia.

All of the willpower and intent that you banked up in your anger, frustration, and regret was spent on making unrealistic proclamations and then fizzled out as you realized you weren't going to make it all happen.

Perhaps it began with missing the gym one day as a work meeting went late.

Then your kid gets sick and misses school.

You get a sitter and make it to the gym! Whew.

But the kid's still got a fever.

You miss a night of sleep, and the kid's home again the next day.

No sleep. No sitter.

Screw the gym . . . You can't do this.

This is the beginning of the end.

You've chucked the gym commitment.

Now it's easy to bail on building the tower, drop your expectations at work, and eat that pumpkin pie that's been taunting you.

It's over.

Date: January 16.

Does this sound like someone you know? Perhaps someone in the mirror?

It's all too common. In fact, it's an epidemic.

Here's why it's bad.

When we bail on an obligation to ourselves, we've just made a journal entry in the book of life. We made a commitment—think back to the words *honor* and *integrity* here—and that commitment is the bond of our word to our very character. It's supposed to be sacred.

Then we break it.

Everyone else is doing it too, so it can't be that bad, right?

By "everyone," do you mean all the hungry ghosts who are spiritually dead inside, making the world look the way it does? They have lost their honor. They are lost souls.

Does that sound mean or too harsh to you?

Tough love. Let's explore.

Breaking the central deal with your spirit not only compromises your *word*, it also proves to your inner self that you have *failed* and can't be trusted. *You can't keep a promise.*

It reinforces the data point: YOU FAIL.

If you keep reinforcing the idea that you fail, each year, one resolution at a time, then you lose all faith in yourself. Your word means nothing. Your commitments can be broken. You can't be trusted.

You start saying things that you don't really mean. Forget about New Year's—it's on a daily basis.

"I'll be there at six" means "I'll get there when I do—probably six forty-five—and you'll wait around for me."

"I do" turns into "I'm getting some side action on business trips because my co-workers do it too . . . I mean, who means it when they take a marriage vow?"

"The check is in the mail" means "I'll pay you when I get paid next Friday. I already spent the money on a new pair of shoes."

Are you catching my drift?

Once you get comfortable lying to yourself, you're much more likely to lie to others. This sets off a chain reaction and gives us the world we live in. If you're constantly complaining about your friends being jerks, take a look at yourself. Is your nose clean?

How can we be accountable to others if we're not accountable to ourselves?

How can we succeed in life if we keep failing ourselves on the "little things"?

There are no little things.

Show me how you do one thing, and I'll know how you do everything.

Part of the work we're doing together is a delicate process of bringing your honor and integrity back into everything that you do.

You do what you say and say what you do.

There's *integrity* in that. When we restore integrity, we stand a chance of winning at the internal and external game of life.

THE EXTERNAL GAME

Sure, we can make a deal with the devil and cheat people out of their money. We can drive fancy cars, have huge houses, buy politicians, and start wars. We've all seen these people on TV. Many of them are completely dead inside. They are estranged from their children, on their fourth marriage, need transfusions to stay alive, or take heavy drugs to sleep at night—all to overpower the scary "thoughts" they can't run from.

These aren't lives that are winning. They're the empty shells that are left after people take the devil's bait.

THE INTERNAL GAME

If you want to master time, get the life you want, and have balance and harmony, you'll need to restore your honor *with yourself.* That's the internal game, and we're here to win it.

In this chapter, we're going to take a deep dive into the concepts of *focus* and *willpower,* or *attention* and *intention.* We're going to look at how the ancient Taoists viewed these forces and see why it's so important to understand them. Our focus determines our reality, and there's an enormous industry out there that's hired teams of neuroscientists who understand your brain and behavior. They are vying for your attention, and, sadly, they're getting it.

Our minds are being mined.

Our life force is being pilfered.

If you want to stand a chance at living a full, meaningful life, you'll need to take back the reins.

ATTENTION IS THE CURRENCY OF THE INFORMATION AGE

The great challenge of our time is the battle raging in the background for the *minds* of humanity. Advertisers compete for "eyeballs," and marketing has gotten so damned sophisticated that we hardly stand a chance.

We have a saying in the martial arts: "If you stand in the ring for long enough, you'll eventually get punched in the face."

That's how I feel about TV. I'm not smart enough to watch it. There are huge rooms filled with researchers who use functional MRIs to map the parts of our brains that light up with different colors, sounds, smells, images, and whatnot. There's a tremendous amount of data that's already been compiled on what makes us tick and tock, what makes us feel insecure and act *predictably* in response to certain stimuli.

We've evolved from generations of more primitive mammals that were simply trying to survive. But have we evolved? We've created a world filled with technology that makes our heads spin, but our biology is effectively the same.

It is *predictably* the same.

Sweet foods, fats, shelter, safety, and the ability to attract a mate are high up in our brain's priorities for life and for survival. This circuitry is well understood and has been hacked to get us to behave as a good consumer, voter, and, well, sheep. Spend your money, pay your taxes, and don't ask too many questions.

As a matter of fact, don't have any dreams. We'll tell you what you want in life.

It's a white picket fence and an SUV.

No?

Oh, it's a Porsche and a young spouse.

Not that either?

Okay, you're a surfer then? Wear this brand, and you'll fit right in with the cool crowd.

Just fall into your bucket, keep buying stuff, and let us tell you what life is all about.

It's the Matrix.

You need to break out of that trap, or you're doomed.

CRISIS OF CONSCIOUSNESS

There was a time not too long ago when people lived in a much more meaningful way. Life was imbued with spirituality, and people looked for meaning in signs and omens. The wind, a raven, a falling leaf at the right moment—everything carried meaning.

But now we've stopped asking the important questions and have fallen into a lull, a sleepy trance where we're stumbling around *passing* time instead of *mastering* time and truly living life. We watch the lives of those we respect on TV and somehow know that we can't be like them. We're not destined to live our dreams and can only pass our time and watch the fortunate few live theirs fully.

This is mental imperialism of the most insidious kind.

We've been duped into believing that we're not special, so we hand over *our power of creation* to those that steer. We willingly give them our time, energy, money, and attention and allow them to drive our consciousness where they will. The "stars" are on TV and not all around us in the majestic night sky.

We've forgotten who we are, where we stand. We've forgotten to look up in awe at the grandeur of the Universe all around us.

Let's come back to you: the center of your Universe. You have the creative potential, energy, and time allotted on this planet to create beautiful and magnificent things. You are a creator who's forgotten almost everything. It's time to come home.

Home is right here and now at the center of your being. Home is this current time and this space where you're sitting or standing. Or perhaps you're lying down or walking.

Where's your body right now, and what's it doing?

Wiggle your toes.

Now your nose.

That's it.

Let's start there. You're in your body now, and before your attention gets drawn off again, pucker your lips, furrow your brow.

How long can you stay here?

This question will determine how well you'll be able to manifest a life you want.

Many people may have already come and gone three times since reading "furrow your brow." That's how fickle our attention is. We can't even stay focused for a few moments, let alone on *specific* plans and dreams for our lives.

Is it any wonder that our lives don't work?

We're here to fix that. There's a solution, and you are the central character of this act. Yes, you.

Nobody can do it for you. I certainly can't. But I can point you in the right direction.

Our consciousness has been fragmented, hacked, stolen, manipulated, and diverted, but only because *we've allowed it.*

We didn't know any better.

Now that we do, it's on us to get back in the driver's seat.

If energy is the currency of life and time is the measure of how long we get to live it, then consciousness is the fruit of our labor. We pump blood, consume food, walk around doing things, and somehow, we're *aware* that things are happening.

What is this awareness?

The most important question to ask yourself is this: *"Who am I?"*

The question that follows is even more important: *"Who just asked that question?"*

How are we aware that we exist? What is this existence that we are experiencing? How the heck are we alive, and where did we come from?

This is the stuff religions of the past were born from. Somehow, some Roman dudes compiled a bunch of trite "answers" and put them in holy books and handed them out to everyone. Worse yet, they forced the books, at the point of a sword, on the perfectly happy "pagans" of Europe and then carried those messages to the far corners of the earth, "saving" the heathens by telling them what the answers were and taking away the most important part of the equation: *the inquiry.*

The questions are more important than the silly answers our brains can conjure up, let alone the ones written by imperialists whose aim is to subdue.

The inquiry is the name of the game.

If we don't question, then we're lulled to sleep. If we don't explore the Universe with childlike curiosity, we accept the answers that we're given and live a life of mediocrity.

Consciousness is just a word.

The *exploration* of our consciousness and what it means to be alive—that's the fun part, and that's the part that'll unlock your mind and free your spirit.

In my opinion, this is the most rewarding and therapeutic work you can do with your time. The inner realms have all the answers, and study after study has shown how meditation and internal work can help alleviate pretty much all the psychological stress we suffer from today. Journeys into the inner realms with ayahuasca and Native American rituals can turn around some of the worst addictions.

The workshop is your body.

The workshop is your life.

Your eyes need to turn inward.

SCREEN TIME

I'm not sitting here right now writing these words with a pen and a pad. I'm doing it on a screen. I've written all my books on computers and have a tremendous appreciation for what they can do.

That said, if we're not careful, it's a deal with the devil.

The esoteric Tarot comes from an ancient tradition of early religions of Egypt, carried into the Hermetic and Rosicrucian traditions of Christianity and the Kabbalah of Judaism. It lives on in Sufism and many other traditions around the world. It's deep and profound. Whether you choose to believe in this stuff doesn't matter to me. The allegory is what's important for our insight here.

Major Arcanum #15 of the Tarot is called "The Devil," and it's all about our misunderstanding of who we truly are. All the Devil can do is to trick us and divert our attention away from our pure, essential spiritual nature by distracting us and burying us in drama and confusion. He can contort our understanding of ourselves so that we help co-create the reality he wants outside of God's plan. Now, some would argue that it's all in God's plan, and I tend to agree, but this struggle between God and the Devil for our attention can also be seen as an allegory for human choice.

The Lucifer Experiment was when God's brightest angel thought he could do it better and coerced all of us fallen stars, or angels, to co-create a false reality with him. It's an esoteric explanation of why this world has so many problems—because we're spiritual beings stuck in Lucifer's realm and forced to confront our shadows to wake up to who we truly are.

Here's a key point: we, not the Devil or any outside force, are the ones plugging our creative principle and power into creating the world around us. It's a collective illusion that we are blindly propagating.

We are being distracted and coerced into doing so because our *attention* is being drawn somewhere.

According to the Catholic scholar Valentin Tomberg, author of *Meditations on the Tarot*, the Devil's signature energy is "electrical." This has powerful implications for where we stand in our world. Again, I'm writing this book on a laptop. It's connected to the internet.

Where are our eyes being drawn off to?

Just reach into your pocket. Look at your desk and find a monitor. Most living rooms feature a big TV as the central feature nowadays.

We're addicted to our screens. We're constantly checking the news, sports scores, weather, and the like. And another insidious area has emerged: social media.

Social media is sucking the attention right out of our lives and distracting us with noise and nonsense. Stanford scientists have helped the social media companies create powerfully addictive apps that keep us engaged and check-ing our feeds hundreds of times a day.

They all dance to the tune of money, and the allure of being the next tech billionaire has smart people at these companies jumping in with both feet and looking away from the implications of what they are doing.

They are monetizing our eyes and attention and buying private jets. They are manipulating sentiment and winning elections. They are stoking fear, racism, and consumerism, all in the name of progress.

Some of social media can be argued to be good, and I would agree. But what about the rest?

Our attention has been pulled into a false reality that's using our base survival instincts and circuitry to spend, vote, and believe certain things about the world. Our souls are neglected, and our dreams and aspirations get shoved aside as the next big thing, event, trend, or drama jumps in front of us.

We are behaving exactly like the Buddhists said. We're being hungry ghosts—or perhaps more like zombies unable to think for ourselves any longer.

Our attention has become the currency of the information age.

Information is the new medium, and particular value is being placed on its interpretation and curation for people who don't have time to research things on their own.

In this new information age, curators, thought leaders, authority sites, and news sites (real and fake) become the arbiters of information. People go there to figure out what's going on, and the sites need to monetize that attention, so they either sell stuff directly or rent out ad space to others who are selling stuff.

This incessant competition for our attention is a multi-billion-dollar industry, and the household names of Google, Microsoft, Amazon, and Apple are all collecting data on our behavior and selling it to companies that have a vested interest in knowing how we feel, what we like, and what news interests us.

Our behavior is being mapped for clues about where we may buy something next. It's ingenious if you think about it—the natural expression of advertising science. But, alas, it's gotten out of hand.

This neuroscience-inspired industry understands us more than we understand ourselves—and, more importantly, it understands how this messaging can supplant our priorities and distract us away from the things in life we say we value.

BACK TO THE GARDEN

If you're leaking Water left and right to social media here and "retail therapy" there, you may be surprised at how little time, energy, and money you have left to hatch your dreams. It seems innocuous at first, but when you look at the global impact on all areas of your life, there's a lot being wasted on screen time and media.

Where's the silence and tranquility we need to manifest a rich and meaningful existence?

It's eluding us and feeding someone else.

Someone who gets to live their dreams because we're providing the fuel for them.

Let's take a deeper dive into the anatomy of conscious-ness from a Taoist perspective. As a Taoist abbot, that's the tradition I hail from.

Taoism is the philosophy of balance and harmony with nature and comes from ancient China. Taoist practitioners are adept at the internal arts. That means we spend lots of time meditating and focusing our breath on different areas in our body. The Taoist understanding of internal energetics birthed acupuncture and Chinese herbology, which have helped billions of people. They are among the safest and most effective forms of natural medicine we have.

To understand life, we need to understand the flow of energy, the currency of life. It's very much like the old detective wisdom on solving crimes—"follow the money."

For us to take back our attention and use it to help water our Life Garden, it's important to understand the fundamentals of how these forces work within our minds and bodies, including our deep and subtle psychology.

THE ANATOMY OF CONSCIOUS MANIFESTATION

We've learned that attention and intention (also called focus and intent) need to be coupled in order to manifest things in life, so let's take a look at the 5,000-year-old system of energetic understanding that explains this.

Mind you, this information comes from centuries of Taoist alchemical exploration, study, and confirmation among practitioners. This stuff isn't theory; it's time tested and well understood by adepts of the various Taoist traditions that remain on the planet. In fact, it's millennia older than the United States of America and the European countries that preceded the U.S. in the Western world. The people that pooh-pooh it may have an agenda, and it's not your best interest they're defending; it's a restrictive worldview based on dogma and religious/medical control.

JING, QI, AND SHEN

The foundation of what you're about to learn is what we Taoists call the "Three Treasures"—*Jing*, *Qi*, and *Shen*. These Treasures are the main ingredients of the internal arts, and each is to be cultivated for health, vitality, and the expansion of our consciousness.

As a metaphor, we can look at a candle. The wax would be the Jing, the fire would be the Qi, and the halo, or glow, around the flame would be the Shen. Let's look at each more closely.

Jing

Jing is the essence of the body. It's what we inherit from our parents via our DNA, and it's the hand of cards we're dealt when incarnating on planet Earth. We're born with this "Treasure" and need to protect and cultivate it throughout our lives. This is the candle most of us burn through in our youth that doesn't come back. We can do practices like yoga, Qigong, Tai Chi, and meditation to help offset its loss, and we can refine it into the other two Treasures, but it's hard (if not impossible) to put back into the bank.

Jing needs to be conserved and not squandered. Excessive sexual activity, late nights, stimulant abuse, stress, and activities that overly tax the body and mind are all culprits in the depletion of Jing. The Jing is housed in the kidneys (and adrenals) and associated with the Water element.

Qi

Qi is the energy of life. It's ignited by our Jing and derived from the combination of food and air. It's the metabolic energy that runs our life, the "currency" of life we've been talking about. It powers our organs and our immunity, fires our neurons, and, frankly, keeps the lights on. Qi is the fuel for life, and we run on it daily.

If the body is the vehicle, the Qi is the power coming from the combustion of gasoline. That power is only moving when the "engine" is "on," so there's no Qi when the car isn't running.

When Qi is depleted, we're exhausted. When it's full, we have energy, optimism, a firing brain, and a healthy sex drive.

In the clinic, when patients would tell me they had no time, I'd often equate that to them having no energy. They were depleted in Qi, and their life wasn't working because it lacked the juice needed to run correctly. But some simple lifestyle changes can crank up our Qi and make enormous changes in our lives.

Shen

Shen is the spirit. It's the payload, or outcome, of a life lived correctly. It also translates as "Mind" and is housed in the heart. The Shen flowers through the eyes, which are the gateway to the spirit, and it works in two ways. The Shen is directed where we focus our eyes, and our eyes are also a reflection of our healthy spirit. Have you ever met someone and immediately known that something was very wrong with them because their eyes were dead and flat? That's a reflection of their Shen.

When the Shen is vibrant, you can see the twinkle in someone's eye. You can see life coursing through them. Shen is rich and robust in enlightened masters, whose eyes speak volumes so they don't need to.

The focused direction of our Shen, or our attention, will be a point of continual importance.

Fusion of the Three Treasures

The Jing is the base of the body's energy systems, the Qi is the currency, and the Shen is the afterglow.

It is said that the Qi follows the Shen, and that is how the material world assembles around us.

Think about the implications of this.

Where you focus your mind and guide your spirit with your eyes will direct the energy of your life, and that energy will reinforce a pattern that will eventually settle into a material reality.

Your focus determines your reality.

So if your eyes are engaged in social media all day, your spirit is scattered in cyberspace.

When you close your eyes and turn your attention to your breath or an internal area of your body, the energy flows inward again—watering your fields, your organs, your dreams and aspirations.

In my tradition we call it "Retroflection," the art of turning the light of awareness inward and growing its glow. You can learn more about this in detail by reading *The Secret of the Golden Flower* by Lü Tung-pin, the founder of my lineage.

This is an important principle we'll come back to as we reclaim our eyes and attention. Turning our awareness inward is the beginning of a powerful shift in orientation, one that will help you come back to life and reclaim your personal power.

TAOIST ALCHEMY

In my tradition, the ultimate goal of the work is the fusion of Heaven and Earth within our bodies. This is where the fun really starts. It's all about taking the fragmented pieces of our existence and bringing them home, here and now. It is about being fully alive and aware in this moment and realizing the magnitude of who we truly are. We're spirits living in a material existence, and when we reconcile the polarity of our understanding of this, we become whole.

There is no Heaven versus Earth. It's all here now, and our consciousness is split. We need to wake up to the Unity of our existence. There's no either/or.

The way this plays out is in our lives. In our bodies, Heaven is represented by the Fire element, and Earth is represented by the Water element. It may be a little confusing because there's also a separate "Earth" element, but here we're talking about the big-picture Heaven and Earth instead of the element Earth.

The Fire Element

The Fire element is housed in the heart and is the energy of our Shen, our pure, undifferentiated spirit that connects us with all Life and the Universe. It's the eternal part of us that lives on and loves all. The heart houses our Attention, as it's the seat of our Shen. It's our focus and what we refer to as our Mind here in the West.

It's our connection to Heaven and the root of our passion, creativity, and loving kindness.

The Fire of the Heart is the element tied to our *focus,* or *attention*. It's also associated with Time.

See! It comes back around.

The Water Element

The Water element is tied to what's called our *Zhi*, or our *intent*.

And we've come full circle!

It's anchored in our material existence, the *space* that we live in. Our Jing, or essence, helps power it, and that's why it's so important to save and not squander it. Water is our connection with our material existence as coded in our DNA, and it's dynamically balanced with Fire. Our drive, or willpower, is the battery at the core of our existence that wills things into being, and it's a force we've fallen out of sync with.

This element relies on our Jing, and our hectic, fast-paced lifestyles have been draining this force for some time. We muster it up and try to force things to happen, but each year it's harder, as our Vitality is diminished.

The Water of the kidney is associated with our *willpower*, or intention. It's our anchor into *space*.

Making Steam

The fusion of Fire and Water gives us steam, the mixing of the elements in perfect harmony. My Taoist school is a "Steam School," and many of our internal practices cultivate this reality inside the body.

Steam is the fusion

of *Time* and *Space*,
of *Attention* with *Intention*,
of *Focus* and *Willpower*.

It's the missing ingredient in our lives when it comes to manifesting and watering our Life Garden. Without understanding the essential "spiritual science" of how we function, we're lost and wandering out there. From the Masons to the Sufis to the Kabbalists, every tradition has some of this wisdom on lock, and when you look at who's diving into it, there are some pretty prominent people.

Why? Because it's true.

HOW I GOT HERE

It seems like a miracle how all of this came together in my life. I was studying the inner alchemical work with my masters and then learned the process of Gongs from another teacher. I experimented with Gongs and began to understand that the principles I was working on in my internal work lined up perfectly with the Life Garden work I was "stumbling upon."

It then dawned on me. If something is true and pure, it should apply across the board to all things as a universal principle. This real-world understanding of these alchemical secrets snuck up on me and taught me how the internal work and external work are not different at all. In fact, how can they be?

Several aha moments have dawned on me over the decades of doing this work. My understanding continues to grow and to get deeper in layers.

There's only one reality.

Our fragmented and distorted understanding of reality makes things seem separate. But they are not.

As you do this work, you will align your inner reality with your outer. When there's no distinction, you'll know you're getting there. When you see unity in all things, you become whole and enlightened.

You become a wizard.

Please be a good one.

THE ART OF MANIFESTATION

I've been an expert manifester since I left the monastery. My internal state goes still, and then I see my Life Garden, and shortly thereafter, my life reflects what's in my vision. I've written multiple books, made several films and series, traveled the world, and I have a great family and live on a ski mountain. I've conjured up a great life doing this work and am grateful for all the blessings. I'm here to teach that art of manifestation to you.

You are a creator dreaming a dream.

How clear can you be, and how much amplitude can you put behind the signal? .

That's really the name of the game.

Think of a radio broadcast station. It gets tuned to a specific frequency and then pulls power through and broadcasts as far as the power can push it. You need an antenna and a signal to broadcast. As a human, you have both.

Your focus and attention are like the frequency, and your willpower and intention push the power.

Now, a lot of this depends on how much personal power you are able to access. That's why I cannot overemphasize the importance of health and Vitality. Your body is the battery that powers your dreams; it's hard to push a strong signal without the juice to back it.

We'll come back to practices that'll boost your Vitality in a later chapter. Right now, we're looking at what it takes to manifest. Once you understand the ingredients (which are pretty simple), then you can prioritize how to enhance your access to both.

Focus and clarity come from meditation, Qigong, Tai Chi, yoga, prayer, and dedicated quiet time. They come from "taking your eyes back" from the electronic world of devices and screens and turning them inward to silence the reactivity of the mind and explore inner realms. Your focus is also a central player in the work we're about to embark on with the creation of your Life Garden.

In the previous chapter, we mapped out your current situation. Now I'm taking some time to explain how this all works so that, when you're ready, you can roll up your sleeves and map out what you'd like your Life Garden to look like in the next 30, 60, and 100 days. What about life in one year? Five years?

This is all up to you, but once you've decided, it'll take focus and clarity to stay on path. It'll also take willpower and intention to drive your personal power and water all those plants.

MUSTERING WATER

With Water being the combined resources of time, energy, and money, we actively trade one for another and can use them together or separately to feed different areas of our Life Garden.

We'll now start working on a strategy to enhance the flow of your Water and increase the amount you have access to. Again, this comes from lifestyle, a magical word that gets overlooked all too often.

Vitality is about *how* we live. In the next chapter, we're going to analyze our personal "Energy Economics" and get better at understanding where we're losing Water and where we can easily muster up some more.

The Pareto principle implies that 80 percent of our results come from 20 percent of our efforts. So what knobs can we turn that will crank out more Vitality for us?

What class or commitment can we cut that'll give us the time we need to exercise?

What toxic friends can we avoid so we can get more quality time with our families?

All of this calculus gets factored into our Energy Economics as we figure out how to best nurture and maintain our Life Garden.

ADJUSTING THE SPRINKLERS

When I was in my teens and twenties, I had too much energy. If I watered my Garden, it came through as flood irrigation. Abundant Water poured recklessly around the vicinity of a plant. Everything around it grew, including the weeds. So long as I focused on something now and again, things would get done thanks to the sheer volume of Water I could spare.

Then the thirties came. Life, school, and career drained my reserves, and the Water started to diminish. Fatigue became a thing—not terrible but certainly a new, unwelcome friend. By my late thirties, I painfully learned my lesson and shifted to a regular sprinkler system. Essentially, the sprinkler head would putt around from left to right and try to water everything in each pass.

This was a much more efficient way of watering plants, but it still wasted some Water and watered weeds all around.

It wasn't until my forties that I got tactical. Think drip irrigation, the most efficient way to grow crops. You have a dedicated line dripping Water to each plant in your Garden, with a valve that adjusts volume individually. You can get very clear on which plants need more Water right now and which you can minimally sustain.

The benefit was that I didn't have withering or dead plants in some areas and thriving ones in others. The key was to move the whole Garden along while emphasizing specific plants at certain intervals.

Think about it. Perhaps your career is taking off right now. That's great, but it can't come at the expense of your health or your marriage. Now think about it in terms of Water allocation.

How can you drip Water to the areas that need to be fed without making it just lip service? It's easy to say you're hanging out with your kids when you're actually at the kitchen table digging into emails. It's easy to think you're being healthy by ordering the occasional salad while skipping the gym for weeks on end.

Honesty is needed.

Refer back to your list of which areas you're skimping on and which ones need more love. Which ones are getting over-watered, and which are getting underwatered?

When our Water is emptied, we feel depleted. We don't have enough to go around, so we cheat. We pilfer from here and there to keep "critical systems" running. That's like a country cutting the budget for teachers, books, hospitals, and the arts in order to save money. In the long run, society crumbles under the weight of this.

Now, I understand that you may feel exhausted and defeated already, and it's hard to map out a bright future when you can't see or feel it.

You need more Water. In times of drought, rain is godsent.

So let's make it rain. But before we do so, let's make sure you know how to avoid squandering it all.

REINVESTING YOUR WATER

You may not feel very vibrant right now. That's fine. It's a result of poor Energy Economics and a lack of Water to draw from. Of course you feel that way.

In a cracked, barren desert landscape, things don't flow right with lack of moisture. But when it finally rains, the soil sucks every last bit of that Water and out sprouts life again. This will start happening in your life shortly. You'll begin to feel better and have more energy.

Don't squander it.

When I was in Oriental medical school, I was also train-ing as a monk in my lineage. I would study hard and take a quarter off each year to go on sabbatical. I got to study with the Dalai Lama, the Karmapa Lama, and a whole host of amazing teachers.

One year, I was taught a particular practice and was to perform certain austerities before doing the practice in isolation for a couple of weeks. I went deep into Waimea Canyon on the Hawaiian island of Kauai. There wasn't a soul around for miles. I water fasted for five full days before performing the practice—the cultivation of breath, energy, and light.

When I came back home and met with one of my attending doctors, she took a look at me and smiled. She said I looked wonderful—years younger and full of light. I blabbed on about how amazing I felt and how powerful and meaningful it was, and I'll never forget the advice she gave me:

"Don't spend it."

Huh?

"Just don't spend it all."

Three weeks later I was mired in the daily rounds of patient care, dealing with exams, and caught up in some drama. I walked into my attending doctor's class, and after taking a look at me, she shook her head. "You spent it!"

She was right. I was such an idiot. I didn't keep any of that energy for myself, and certainly none for a rainy day. In my desire to be liked, loved, and respected, I showered all that energy on everyone around me and forgot to keep some/most/any for my own Life Garden.

Please don't do that.

As we grow in this work, I know that you'll start feeling better. Please take some of that newfound energy and Vitality and invest it into more lifestyle interventions that'll keep eking out more Water for you.

Your Energy Economics will need to be adjusted for better efficiency. If you barely have enough mojo to get through your days right now, how the hell are you going to manifest anything meaningful in the future?

We'll work to fix that, and as you feel better, I ask you not to squander all your Water on weeds in your Garden. There are important plants that are starving for the Water. With the proper balance, all these areas will start to thrive and demonstrate an important principle: *life begets life*.

GOOD SOIL

Any good gardener knows that once certain plants get healthy and begin to blossom, the magic begins. The soil gets healthier, and the microbes and worms in the soil start to thrive. That creates the raw substrate for the other plants to also thrive. And once the soil bounces back, something very powerful and relevant happens to it.

Healthy soil is filled with healthy commensal bacteria. In a way, this soil takes on a life of its own, and here's the kicker: it begins to *retain water*.

There are huge implications in this for us.

As we get better at watering the plants in our Gardens, they push up and down at the same time. They develop healthier roots and root nodules. The bacterial life that thrives in the *soil* of our Life Garden then helps the other plants thrive, and a symbiotic and synergistic effect takes place.

You can start with cracked, unhealthy soil around a couple of wilting plants and have a thriving biosphere within months once you're playing the game right. Healthy soil retains water better.

This is exactly how it works in our lives. Hermes Trismegistus famously said, "As above, so below."

Our lives mirror the natural world all around us. The inner and outer worlds are one. As we begin to garden our lives and bring Water and life to the critical areas, certain efficiencies show up. We start to feel better and invest some of that energy into other areas of life.

A prime example of this is diet and exercise. If you clean up your diet, you start having more energy. Eventually, you'll feel like exercising, so you start with long walks, and then jog, and eventually you're back in basketball. All this exercise has powerful benefits for your nervous system, so now you're less stressed and sleeping better. This helps you have more energy, which you invest in a hiking trip, and you find yourself making moves at work. Sales are up, and money is better. You take your family on a long-needed vacation, and things start to mend in that area. It's a positive upward spiral of healthy soil that continues to feed upon itself in your Garden.

OUR MIND'S SOIL: THE SUBCONSCIOUS MIND

The ancient traditions have a general framework for different aspects that come into play in the anatomy of our consciousness. Remember, before the modern era, humanity had multiple traditions that spent countless hours exploring the inner realms. Millions of people over the millennia sat in monasteries, tuned their consciousnesses inward, and mapped this out for us. They recorded it and shared it, gifting it forward to us.

The essential understanding of consciousness is needed to map out our trajectory. Intention and Attention are absolutely the key seeds for life that must be watered.

That's *almost* it, but the magic happens *in the soil*.

Our subconscious mind is the soil in which our ideas get watered, nourished, and hatched. This is the level right under the surface that takes suggestions from our conscious mind and works on them while our conscious focus is doing its thing elsewhere.

Here's an image from my first book, *Inner Alchemy*, where we spend a good deal of time on this topic.

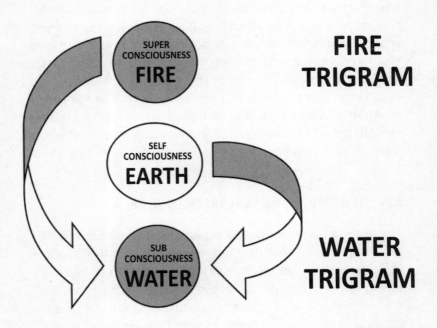

There's a lot happening here, and I recommend reading *Inner Alchemy* after this book to better understand the esoteric stuff. For our purposes, I'll dive into the broader ideas here.

Our *superconscious mind* is the part of our consciousness that's connected to the divine/Universal intelligence. It's associated with *Fire* or *Heaven* energy. It's our direct link to all the intelligence in the Universe—all of it. This is the mind we would like to tap into so we can take divine inspiration into our daily lives. As we further align with our purpose, we're more in tune with this intelligence and in the flow.

Our *self-conscious mind* is where we live. It's the mind we live in and operate with daily. We drive, read, make decisions, and basically run all our *earthly* affairs from this aspect of our consciousness. It's where all the surface action is—our sense of self, our ideas about what to do today, and so on.

Our *subconscious mind* lies below the surface. It's tied to the *Water* element. It is the essential nature of who we are. It is the Jing, the intuition, the subtle layers of our being, and the soil in which ideas germinate and sprout into life. It's what's running all the time, taking information from and feeding information into our Conscious mind. Just as with the soil, all the action is happening below the surface. The soil is filled with life, and the healthy expression of this life makes the plants thrive above the surface.

Our minds work the same way.

Both the superconscious and self-conscious minds feed information to the subconscious mind, and the subconscious mind also feeds information back to the self-conscious mind.

This puts our subconscious mind in a unique position to both receive and transmit information. This is where a great deal of trauma, bad habits, negative beliefs about ourselves, and faulty memes are harbored and deeply embedded.

A meme is a mental virus. An example would be "Money is evil" or "You'll never amount to anything." They can be pushed into us by others, like "Immigrants are dangerous" or "[this race] is lazy." Consider them seeds of thought or belief that live in the soil of our subconsciousness and keep drawing water off our Vitality. They sneak in under the radar and embed into the rich soil of our subconscious mind, where they fester and grow weeds.

Unless we learn to examine and clear these negative beliefs from the soil of our being, we'll continue to blindly water them and wonder why our lives don't work. On the flip side, as we get better at understanding our inner realms, we wipe the soil clean of these nasty bugs and start to embed healthy ones.

An example would be weeding the "Money is evil" meme and replacing it with one that programs the thought "I attract richness and abundance to me effortlessly." One of these programs will help you stop sweating your bills. What'll it be?

The subconscious soil of your mind is where we make or break an intentional life. It's the place where you'll be doing meaningful work in the future.

ENERGY ECONOMICS

You're going to need energy to nourish the seeds you've planted. You'll need Vitality and motivation. The fusion of Intention and Attention is powerful and can move mountains, but only if there's some power behind it.

As you continue on this journey, keep in mind that there may be some toxic negative beliefs embedded in your subconscious that keep getting you to sabotage your progress. Be vigilant and mindful of them. As they come up, jot them down, and we'll make a plan to work on replacing them.

LIFE GARDENING HOMEWORK

Now that we have a better understanding of how the mind works, it's time to dive into your current relationship with the elements at play. As we've learned, each area of the mind is important for manifestation in our lives, so let's look at them individually and jot down some notes.

INTENTION

Where have you been successful with willpower and intention in your life?

Where have you come up short?

What's kept you from mustering power for your endeavors?

What can you do in the future to muster more resources for your dreams?

Where does most of your energy go right now?

Where do you think you can consolidate and gather more power?

ATTENTION

How good has your focus been in the past?

When do you tend to get distracted?

What draws your eyes off your goals?

Have you been good about setting goals?

Are your goals clear and well defined?

Do you give yourself enough time to focus on your goals? Daily? Weekly?

Do you have a practice designed to hone your attention?

SUBCONSCIOUS PROGRAMMING

What negative memes can you identify in your subconscious that may not be serving you?

How much of your behavior could be coming from these memes?

What can they be replaced with?

What other subtle programming can you place into your subconscious mind that may help you along your journey?

CHAPTER FOUR

ENERGY ECONOMICS

When I first left my monastic training and began to teach students the practices I know, I set myself up for some powerful life lessons, none of which were anticipated and several of which were not quite what I'd call fun. I jumped into teaching wholeheartedly and thought that the energy yoga practices I was sharing would do nothing but help people. They would enhance lives, bring peace and happiness to the world, and fa la la.

Nope.

I was wrong.

After the first few months, I noticed that certain students were starting to spin out of control. They were gaining more health and Vitality at first, but then came trouble.

The weeds in the garden were taking over.

The more they upped their power, the more chaotic their lives became. They made some terrible decisions or squandered their newfound energy on lifestyle choices that didn't serve them.

Their chaos was suddenly backed by more power—it raised the amplitude.

My students were the "cash meets energy" equivalent of lottery winners. If you have bad spending habits, the money will be gone in a few months or years, and you'll likely be right back where you started, or possibly worse. Many lotto winners end up in worse debt, or their lives fall apart because they amplify all their bad habits, which are newly fueled by money, which is a form of energy.

As far as my Qigong students go, this obviously didn't happen to everyone. The vast majority of people did great, but a select handful got more chaotic. I don't like failing people, so I got to work trying to figure out what was happening.

These people were spinning out of control in a variety of ways. They'd have more sexual virility and then get into trouble. They'd gain more mental clarity and start to manipulate people around them. They'd take their new energy to dance parties and mix it with drugs.

Why was something as innocuous as energy yoga messing people up?

I kept digging in the ancient manuscripts and learned that the masters of old knew all about this. They'd seen it in each new generation. It turns out that our fundamental operating system is much like a thermostat. It'll always revert to what it was set to. Unless we adjust the dials, we will revert to the earlier settings.

There's also a cache of unresolved drama and trauma we've all buried. More energy tends to dislodge this stuff. We need to be prepared to metabolize it instead of burying it. This takes maturity and commitment. It means being willing to deal with the uncomfortable baggage of the past while working to forgive, come whole, and get real with ourselves.

My studies eventually evolved into a lecture series I developed called "Energy Economics." It's since helped thousands of people and continues to evolve. Let's explore this topic now, as it's likely the missing link for you if you keep playing yo-yo with your goals in life. It also corresponds directly with your energy levels.

You need energy to play the game of life. In fact, when we look at the Life Garden, if the Health area is not vibrant, there's less energy to go around for everything else. We lag, we borrow from other Garden areas, and we cheat with stimulants and shortcuts. None of this is sustainable.

On the other hand, more energy on top of a powder keg of repressed emotions will eventually lead to an explosion, and usually not a pretty one.

A balance of Energy Economics is what actually works.

BALANCING YOUR ENERGY ECONOMICS

A company has a number of departments that all need to function together in some manner. You can't have a strong sales department selling things the factory can't produce on time. You need human resources, customer service, shipping and fulfillment, and a whole host of other departments to work right in order to run a healthy and profitable company. Our bodies work the same way in many regards, and in this chapter, we're going to take a deep dive into the various "departments" that beget Vitality.

Vitality is the end result of the areas of Diet, Exercise, Sleep, and Mindset all working together in a healthy, balanced way. You can't be doing well in one or two of these categories while doing terribly in the others. All the parts make up the whole.

Without your health, your Life Garden is running on mere life support. You're dripping a little here and there to keep things alive, but your Garden is not vibrant and thriving. That's an issue if you have unfulfilled dreams and aspirations.

If you want to master time and hone your focus on the dreams you'd like to sprout in this life, you have to have energy.

Energy comes from *how we live*. That's lifestyle. A healthy lifestyle begets Vitality, which *fuels* a full and meaningful life.

How we get there may be different for each of us, as we've all arrived here along unique paths with unique histories. That said, in my clinical experience, over 90 percent of the patients I saw who had significant pathology and complicated diagnoses saw amazing results following the path of simplicity.

We often tend to think that the solution to our complicated lives and complex problems needs to be complicated as well. *I'm such a tangled mess that it'll take teams of people to fix me . . . Nobody knows the trouble I feel . . .*

What if the answer to all this complexity is simplicity?

Our bodies evolved around some simple and predictable forces that had checks and balances built in. As we moved further away from daily exposure to nature, we spun out, and now we're a hot mess.

Nature is simple and elegant.

Our bodies come from Nature.

Let's return to simplicity.

We are going to explore each of the four areas that contribute to our overall Vitality. Each is important in its own right, and each needs to be balanced and enhanced in order to fuel the system as a whole. You may think that you're doing well in one or more of these areas and can skip them over, but please don't.

Keep spinning the wheels that are working okay while focusing on the busted ones. They all need to be spinning. That's the key. We don't want to divert all our attention to one area that needs it and forget the others. This sort of allocation of energy and attention is what harms us. We need to keep our eyes on the big picture and work to bring all areas into balance.

Diet

"You are what you eat" is often looked at as old news, but it's true. Forget all the tabloid-inspired fad diets out there. These outlets need to say something new each week, or else you'll stop reading them.

A good diet is really pretty simple.

Our bodies evolved eating natural foods that came directly from planet Earth. The more we've moved away from that, the sicker we've become. Diabetes, obesity, auto-immune diseases, and neurodegenerative disorders are killing our society and can be helped with healthy diets.

We can change our direction starting today.

Right now.

We are only consuming about 10 percent of the fiber our ancestors used to get from diets that predominantly contained fruits, vegetables, nuts and seeds, whole grains (which came later), and lean meats.

Our microbiomes developed around that kind of diet. Trillions of bacteria, protozoa, viruses, parasites, and nematodes have co-evolved in a symbiotic relationship with us over this time. We fed them lots of fiber from natural sources, and they helped us metabolize the food; produced vitamins, enzymes, and co-factors; and provided us with frontline immune defense. It's a miraculous symphony in our guts that's triggered by the kinds of food we eat.

With modernization and factory food production, we've added pesticides, toxic chemicals, and a lot more refined sugar to that mix. This is feeding the wrong kinds of bacteria to our bodies and throwing off life's balance. Bad bacteria and fungi thrive on sugars and produce by-products that compromise our immunity, cause us to gain weight, and give us neurological disease. It's bad.

We've cut off millions of years of evolution with our technological "advancement," and now we're paying the price.

Food shouldn't make us tired.

Food shouldn't make us sick.

Food is supposed to give us energy and nutrients. It should feed the commensal bacteria in our guts and fuel our whole body to run, jump, read, and think.

If it doesn't, we've got work to do.

Clean up your diet, and only eat things that come from nature. That means they grew out of the ground or on a tree. If you eat animals, eat only ones that lived on a pure, natural diet.

Our bodies don't recognize the millions of new chemical additives we've "enhanced" our food with and can often mount immunity against them in an attempt to protect us. You know from having had the flu how tired you can feel when your immune system is hard at work trying to clear out invaders. Now imagine your body doing that with every meal. This causes a low-grade exhaustion that you can help avoid by eating only organic and natural foods.

Step away from all processed foods, and you're 80 percent of the way there. I mean it. Most people try this for a week and say, "Yeah, I think it helped a little." That's cute. Do it for the rest of your life. Each month, you'll be better, cleaner, happier, and a little bit more whole. Each year, you'll be better than that. It keeps going if you stay with it. That's the problem: we're fickle, and we revert back to the easy way of doing things.

Eat lots of fresh vegetables daily, and mix up the colors.

Have at least two different-colored veggies with each meal, and be mindful of the glycemic index of the fruits you eat. The key is to minimize sugar and maximize fiber. This will feed the right bacteria and get you off the sugar roller coaster. The various colors found in fruits and vegetables contain all sorts of phytonutrients and co-factors that your body needs to run optimally and heal your gut.

When it comes to Energy Economics, the mass consumption of sugar is like trying to live your life on *kindling*, the little scraps of wood you use to start a fire.

A nice, large, sustainable fire needs to be started with kindling, but then the key is to add bigger logs until the fire is burning hot. A good fire can take a huge, damp log and burn it without a problem.

A tiny fire would be snuffed out by this.

That's the big issue with our diets.

An athlete might be able to take down a big, sloppy burrito topped with sour cream, cheese, and red sauce at lunch and not get sleepy, but that's because they have a robust fire that can burn it. But is that you?

If so, then great.

If not, then it's time to rebuild your fire by having smaller meals and stopping eating when you're 50 percent full. Build the fire back up, and not just with kindling or sugars.

If you have problems with proteins, you could consider taking hydrochloric acid and protease as digestive enzymes.

If you have trouble with fats, look at taking lipase.

Carbs? Amylase might work for you.

The issue with carbs is that many people who have compromised digestion think they can only feel okay if they eat carbs. They eat breads, cookies, pastas, and lots of sugar, which gives them short-term energy, but then they crash within 90 minutes.

That's a downward death spiral that I call "deficit spending" in the Energy Economics model.

The key is to help your digestive tract break down the foods you're eating so you can actually extract energy from them. If we go back to the company model, the digestive tract is the receiving department of a company. Its job is to take in checks and process them. That money goes into the bank and fuels the rest of the company's activities, in essence becoming its lifeline.

But what happens if that receiving department sucks at its job? If it's overstaffed and underperforms? Checks sit there, people don't get paid, and the company as a whole lags. People stop coming to work, and everything starts to break. When the digestive tract isn't doing its job to bring in energy, then your body won't have energy to spend. It's simple math.

As Above, So Below . . .

Your digestion needs efficiency. It needs to pull in the good stuff and take in those checks. You need the "money" in your brain and muscles. You need it for your life. This energy is the vital lifeline for all your biological systems, and your gut is where it is supposed to be absorbed.

If your gut is not working well, you can't absorb nutrients and calories efficiently. If you have leaky gut or immunity issues around the gut, you're *spending energy* to fight the food you're taking in, further exacerbating the problem.

Fixing your diet is the fastest way to start feeling more energy.

It starts with cleaning up the source of your food so your body isn't fighting unnatural toxins in your "receiving department." It also has a lot to do with your calorie intake. "Calories in" still can't exceed "calories out" if you want to stay in healthy balance.

That means don't choke out the engine with too much fuel.

It means don't throw the big, wet log on the small fire.

To feel energized, you need a channel of expression. That means finding places to use your energy in ways that beget more energy. Exercise is the gold standard for this, and that's what we'll visit next.

Exercise

Muscle tissue is dense in mitochondria, the little organelles that help us produce energy. If we have more muscle, we have more capacity to produce energy, which allows us to grow and build more muscle.

It's an upward spiral of energy, fitness, mental clarity, and much more. Exercise is the healthiest channel for calories to travel through in order for us to live bigger and healthier lives. Our hearts are big muscles that are also dense in mitochondria.

When we do cardio, we are helping to build the energy-producing qualities of our heart while also propelling nutrients, sugars, and immunity to the whole body with healthy circulation.

A healthy flow of blood and lymph is tantamount to good health and better energy levels.

Building lean muscle mass helps increase our resting metabolic rate, which essentially burns more calories at rest. That's a good thing.

It gives us a healthy channel along which to direct the energy from the food we eat. This way we can eat more, grow more muscle, and produce more energy. This is the energy of life that we can also plug into our Life Garden, and with it our dreams and aspirations. We need the Vitality account overflowing so we can invest our excess energy, or "profits," into other parts of our lives.

This doesn't mean we all need to be massive, buff weight lifters, either. But it does mean we need to build our lean muscle mass and get fit enough to sustain all our metabolic needs and lifestyle goals.

When I have a big project I'm tackling in my business, I make sure I up my fitness routine to match the energy needed to manifest that dream. I run, hike, ski, lift, and bike more to make it happen. This gives me more energy and clarity to get there.

If you have big dreams, you need to slowly build up your campfire until it's a raging bonfire that can light up your life.

We live in a stagnant world, and many of us haven't moved much in years. That's a problem, as this leads to laxity in postural muscles and tightness in others. But if you jump up from that reality and dive for a football, chances are you're going to pull something, which means six months on a sofa and 30 extra pounds to burn off later—not an ideal outcome. I recommend Tai Chi, yoga, or basic functional fitness for most people who are just starting. Slowly build up your movement, and work to build a functional foundation.

Long hikes working up to a moderately high heart rate will get you there. High-intensity interval training will too; just be careful not to hurt yourself. You pull something, and you're out. It's better to start slow and get there when your body is ready. Skiing, basketball, football, rock climbing, Spartan Race, and many other things involve advanced, multiplanar movements and can't be done cold turkey. You need a strong core, balanced leg muscles, a healthy posterior chain, and good flexibility to even attempt this stuff. It may take a month or two to be able to touch your toes, do a minute-long plank, and work on your lunges before you sign up for that race. The challenge is most people in our culture go full "weekend warrior" and jump right into tennis after years of being away. As you get more functionally fit, you can do more. As you do more, higher-intensity exercise can become a reality. When your body is ready, you'll know.

Just keep blowing on the fire and building it up, and you'll be happy you did.

Sleep

Ah, sleep.

Sleep is the wonderful elixir of life that we've kicked to the curb while wondering why we feel so tired and time compressed.

Sleep *happens*.

You don't *do* sleep. You *allow* sleep.

You get out of the way and fall into a restful state of sleep, where the best kind of magic happens. Your body's wisdom takes over—healing, pruning, growing, and restoring.

What goes up must come down, even though we live in a society that values the up exclusively.

Down.

Down.

Down.

That's what's needed for most people who are lacking energy and Vitality. How can you think about a better future if you can barely be here in the present?

Nap when you are tired.

Sleep early and sleep more.

Stop feeling guilty about it.

Get more of it than you think you need.

You've spent your entire life running hard and wonder why you feel tired.

Cheating that fatigue with coffee, pills, uppers, and then downers *borrows from tomorrow's energy today.*

It is not sustainable. Talk about bad Energy Economics!

Sleep fills the tank and restores proper hormone levels of estrogen, estradiol, testosterone, and progesterone. Sex hormones can't balance without good sleep.

It helps adjust leptin and ghrelin levels that modulate appetite.

It replenishes the adrenals that crank all day.

Sleep helps prune neuronal connections that form during the day that we won't need for the next, which helps calm anxiety and worry.

Sleep detoxifies the brain and the cells of the body. We live in such a toxic world that it's hard enough to take out the trash. More toxins and less sleep is a formula for disaster.

It gives us a period when we're fasting to heal cells and slow our burn. We need that for more *sustained* energy all day. The body evolved around these rest and recovery cycles.

Shut it down and go down. That's the simple remedy to the complexity of your day.

I've had hundreds of patients who ate right, exercised, did yoga, and took plenty of ginseng but still didn't feel well. *They were still skimping on their sleep.*

Sure, a better lifestyle may help you need less sleep eventually, but not for a while. In fact, it'll probably take a couple of years to catch up on sleep and start to truly feel alive for most people living in the modern world. Really—this may or may not apply to you, but it is an important reframing. You aren't going to "catch up" on sleep with two weeks in Hawaii. It took a while to get into this mess. It'll take a while to dig out.

Sorry. I know that's not what you want to hear, but I'm here to help you, not blow smoke.

If you want to master time and manifest the life you choose versus the one you simply get, then you'll need Vitality and more Water for your Garden. That doesn't happen without good sleep.

Here are the basics of sleep hygiene:

1. Keep the room cold—68–72 degrees Fahrenheit is ideal for most people.

2. Keep the room dark—get all the lights out of there.

3. No screen time! All devices are unwelcome in the bedroom; get them out.

4. No caffeine after 2 P.M. (or noon if you're sensitive)—the half-life of caffeine keeps cranking up your system for hours after you consume it.

5. No bills or stressors in bed—the bedchamber is for sleep and making love . . . that's it.

Just following these basics can be hard for most people; we've devolved into a lifestyle where we've lost common sense. It's very typical for someone with bad Energy Economics to have another cup of coffee as a "pick-me-up" at 3 P.M. while still at the office. This makes them crave sugar and have a little snack around 4:30, which pushes dinner back to 8:00 or so. Now they've just eaten and need to "relax" by watching some show for an hour or so before going to bed. This pushes bedtime back a couple of hours, and they lie there and try to calm their mind knowing the alarm goes off at 6.

The stress of knowing tomorrow will suck because you can't fall asleep leads to the consumption of sleep aids, which mess with tomorrow's energy, leading to more caffeine use and a downward flush of your energy.

Sound familiar?

We need to address the "operating system" that allows for this kind of slippery life slope. That's next . . .

Mindset

The fourth department we must tend to is Mindset. To me, this is our operating system, our overall attitude in life.

We live in such confusing times. We're bombarded by media messaging that reinforces a narrative that the walls are caving in. Terrorists are out to get us. Foreigners will take our jobs. We're not good enough without a fancy car. The list is endless.

On and on, the messaging makes us feel worried, small, insignificant, and powerless.

That's exhausting.

Worse, if we buy into that worldview, we need to keep up with all the shows on TV, read the news, watch trending videos, and wear the latest fashion.

Well, there goes your sleep.

Exercise? No time for that.

Diet? Who cares? The world is ending.

It's a known fact that people make bad decisions when stressed out and worried. So what does this have to do with health?

It's everything.

Vitality is about *how* we live. Lifestyle is a conscious choice, and we need to make better decisions in a world filled with really bad distractions. If you want to be healthy enough to water your Life Garden and master this game called Life, then you'll need to have your mindset straight. Mindset is the glue that keeps you together.

It starts with choosing to take better care of yourself. If you can't stay focused enough to eat right, how are you going to see impressive, multiyear projects through? You can't and won't. You'll be low on energy, high on stress, lacking sleep, and forgetting to exercise, all of which diminish your Vitality and rob you of the vital "Water" needed to nourish your Garden.

A healthy mindset tells you to go to bed instead of binge-watching another season of some dramatic crap. Space saga? Dragons and elves? Cops? Lawyers? Sexy doctors? It's all the same story line from a couple dozen Greek dramas played out in various settings.

Is that worth your life? Is that how you want to invest your precious heartbeats, or would you rather manifest an amazing life? A healthy mindset is needed to help you make the better choices, the ones that'll actually bring you back to life. I'm not suggesting that you never have fun. In fact, sometimes the right move is to take down a bottle with good friends and dance on the table to loud music—that's a celebration of life. But doing that every night will kill you.

All things in a healthy balance.

Our mindset can also get hijacked by past trauma, when bad memories tied to unresolved emotions come back and haunt us. Trauma can drive irrational behavior, phobias, personality complexes, and full-out panic attacks. It is very real and needs to be dealt with. In fact, there's no running or hiding from trauma, but there's an incredible amount of power trapped in it that we can reabsorb and reintegrate.

You have to clear the past to be capable of being in the present. Staying in the present takes work.

One of the keys to developing and maintaining a healthy mindset and staying in the present is having a meditation practice. This is essential.

Meditation helps calm the mind and allows us to make better decisions. It drives blood and energy to the prefrontal cortex, which is the part of our brain responsible for the negation of impulses, higher moral reasoning, cognitive thinking, and more. This part of our brain basically separates us from the monkeys, and meditation helps enhance its function.

Bad decisions are what have gotten us into this mess. Doesn't it make sense to power up the part of the brain that enhances our focus and clarity? Doesn't it make sense for us to *curate* the life we choose so that we'll have fewer regrets in life?

If you keep saying you want a better life yet are unwilling to do a practice that's proven to help with that, then you're lost.

Come with me if you want to live . . .

> I've done a whole documentary series on the topic of healing trauma and have tapped the best doctors to help my students with its courses and materials. It's real, and there's help and hope for you. Go to theurbanmonk.com for resources on healing trauma.

Vitality

So now we've come full circle. Vitality is the result of the dynamic balance of your Diet, Exercise, Sleep, and Mindset. If you were to give yourself a score in each out of 100, what would it be? I've created a tool to help you assess this, which you can access at theurbanmonk.com/focus.

Your Vitality Score is the average of all four of these numbers. Say you're great in diet but suck with stress; the lower stress number really impacts your overall score in ways that may overpower the high number from diet.

The key is to look at these numbers each month and come up with a plan to bring them all up, hence bringing up your overall Vitality.

This is what leads to good Energy Economics. When each department is profitable with an excess of life, love, and energy, this profit will spill over into other areas and bring up the overall Vitality of your system.

You need the energy.

You need stamina.

Vitality is the basis of the Water we need for our Life Garden. It's what helps us water various areas of our lives.

Without your health and Vitality, this game is just a mental exercise that's cute but won't get results. If you want actual results, you'll need to up your personal power and tune your focus and attention. The focus and attention come from meditation, mind-body practices, and sheer dedication to the life you choose for yourself.

So long as your Energy Economics are off, something will always break.

MORE ENERGY MEANS MORE RESPONSIBILITY

Anyone who has had kids knows that you need to burn off their extra energy at night before bed, or there's going to be sleepless drama. Adults are no different. Excess energy without an outlet is a recipe for trouble.

The goal here is to build Vitality that we invest into our Life Garden. Energy is a gift. You need to plug it into a bigger and more righteous and fulfilling life.

There's a sacred bond with Nature that's carried through our food. The bonds in our food are the energy of the sun trapped in chemical form. We're taking that sunlight and plugging it into our lives, powering our dreams and aspirations. We have a limited amount of time to make our mark on this planet, and then we're gone. We're given the Universe's energy in the form of starlight through our food to do this.

ALLOCATING WATER IN YOUR GARDEN

Managing the flow of your life's Water is a matter of time and energy commitment. Certain things take more time and focus than others. They may be more or less important than others.

The commitment of time is something we've really botched in our daily grind. The cardinal rule of time management is if it doesn't make it onto your calendar, it won't get done—it doesn't exist or matter to you.

Time allocation is a key practice to using your calendar. You have appointments for work, doctors, movies, and whatever else on your phone. Why not for your projects? Why not for your health or dreams?

I always marvel at the disparity in what people say and what they commit to. When I ask patients about their priorities, they list out a bunch of stuff. Then I ask to see their phones. Nothing. Either it's all work stuff or just a few social items, but none of their projects or Life Garden items.

If it's not in there, then when were you going to do it?

When it goes down in your calendar, it becomes a contract with reality. You've carved out actual time in your life— precious heartbeats—to see this thing through. Assuming it's actually important to you, it needs a time allocation to see it become reality. Some things take several months, while others can be done in a few hours total. First, map out your priorities.

Once you've mapped out your priorities, then it's important to assess how much actual time it'll take to see these items through. That's sometimes a sobering wake-up call for people. You can say you want to become a doctor later in life, but have you looked at the actual time commitment to getting that degree? What do you have to let go of to make that happen, and is it worth it? Only you can answer this, but an accurate accounting is essential. You need to be fully honest with yourself.

Once you've done this step, you can decide if each item remains worth it to you. If so, then find the space in your calendar without crowding out the rest of your life, and commit to it. Getting your Life Garden priorities into your schedule is the only way to make sure you see them through.

There are several strategies around setting your priorities. First off, you need a balanced approach so each area of your Garden is watered on a weekly (ideally daily) basis. (That'll come with more clarity when we actually map this out later.) Once we've done this, there are a number of ways to make sure we're tending to each area.

Remember, the Shen drives the Qi, and where this energy flows, matter assembles. Whether your task or project takes a shorter or longer period of time to complete or has a smaller or bigger build, keep your mind stable and energy flowing, and it will happen.

CHUNK TIME

One of the best ways to actually make things happen is to carve out some distraction-free time to focus on one specific item. Two to three hours is about as much as most people can handle in one sitting. A few chunks a week carved out for your projects is a great start. It can cross over into various areas of your Life Garden. For example, a three-hour spot could be called "Date Night" with your spouse, while another may be "Write that Chapter" or "Finish Reports" or "Basketball Night." This helps pepper your calendar with your Life Garden priorities in the different areas. Ideally, there's a nice balance throughout the week for all of these, and you get to water the various areas pretty evenly. A step down from that would be to go heavy on work one week but then balance it out the following week when you can.

This anchors your activities and makes them real commitments in time, and it also helps you see your priorities in writing. If my priorities are not in the calendar and someone asks me what I'm doing on Tuesday, I open it to a blank page and say, "Nothing, let's hang out." But if I put my actual commitments in there, suddenly the day has all sorts of stuff bolted onto it, stuff like "Call Mom," "Take a nap," or "Work out." It can be "soft" things that aren't work stuff but are still commitments. This way you don't cheat yourself.

It's all about being adaptive and knowing that sometimes certain things take center stage. We stay healthy by managing our Energy Economics so we can plug our energy where it's needed, always keeping an eye on our plan and priorities.

MASTERY IS IN THE NEGATION

In many esoteric traditions, there's a similar teaching I've encountered, which essentially says that "mastery is in the negation." The power of the word *no* is the key to your liberation. In the next chapter, we're going to unpack this principle, because saying no is something we're not accustomed to in our world.

We say yes to too many things, not realizing that by doing so, we're saying no to key areas in our Life Garden. We keep taking on new plants and weeds, which effectively chokes out the ones we said we valued.

Let's get into it.

LIFE GARDENING HOMEWORK

Refer back to your Vitality Score from the quiz at theurbanmonk.com/focus. Look at the areas where you're deficient and see how they are draining your overall health and Vitality. It's a big deal, but when we get a handle on where the biggest challenges are in our lives, we know where to start digging the weeds out of our Garden. Right now, I want you to look at each area of your overall Vitality and ask yourself the following questions:

DIET

What would be a couple of easy ways to clean up my diet right now?

What are the worst foods I'm eating? What can I replace them with?

Am I missing meals and then eating in a frenzy?

How many meals am I eating out each week?

What can I do to be better prepared for hunger?

How can I get better in the kitchen?

Are there cookbooks, recipe guides, or other resources I can use to improve my eating? Where can I get them?

Am I eating emotionally? When is it the worst?

What's the hardest meal for me to get right? How can I fix that?

EXERCISE

How many days per week am I getting exercise right now?

Am I working as hard as I could, or am I going through the motions?

Do I have issues with motivation or simply lack the energy to feel like working out? If it's lack of motivation, where is this coming from? What can I do to fix this?

If it's lack of energy, what's happening with my diet, sleep, and stress levels that may be leading to this?

Am I stretching before strenuous activity?

Am I strengthening postural and core muscles as I go?

What's my favorite form of exercise? How can I get more of it?

Where can I wrestle away some time to get in more movement?

Can I get more active at work? How?

What's the main hang-up I have with exercise, and how can I get over it?

SLEEP

Am I going to bed too late?

Do I drink enough water at night?

Am I looking at a screen two hours before bedtime?

Am I taking stressful things to bed with me? How can I avoid that?

Is it cool and dark in my bedroom when I sleep?

Am I having a hard time falling asleep?

Am I getting deep, restful sleep every night?

Am I able to stay asleep through the night?

Do I have to urinate too often at night?

What else may be impacting my sleep?

Am I waking up rested and ready for my day? If not, what can I do to fix that?

MINDSET

Is my attitude getting in the way of my best life? How so?

Is stress making me act impulsively? Where do I see this in my life?

Am I using food or drugs to self-medicate when stressed?

What else do I do when I'm stressed that doesn't serve me?

How can I better cope with the stressors in my life?

What seems to help take the edge off? Is that good for me?

What positive behaviors can I adopt that'll help me have a clear head?

What am I doing to actively combat and manage stress in my life?

Jot down your answers to all of these questions and anything else that comes to mind. We're going to be working to create a plan to improve whatever situation you're in later, but right now, these exercises are designed to help you better comprehend where you stand in each area of your life.

CHAPTER FIVE

WEEDING YOUR GARDEN

In a world where there are too many stimuli, new things to buy, politicians to listen to, advertising ventures into our brains; it's just a matter of time before the walls cave in. It becomes almost impossible to hold the line. What line?

Your line. The line you draw around your sanity, dreams, aspirations, and goals to create the space needed to live your best life.

There are relentless waves of outside influences working to breach your defenses and get you to buy, vote, believe, and act a certain way. The world is filled with competing influences vying for your attention—the prime currency in the information age. We are the bodies the leeches drink from, the carcasses the parasites leave behind after their feeding frenzy.

Sound harsh?

Sorry, I didn't make the rules. The early Gnostics wrote of a parasitic race called the Archons who function like mental vampires and drain us of our life force.

It is our job to hold the line and take a stand for ourselves, or we simply don't stand a chance.

Let's get into how to do that.

THE PROBLEM WITH THE WORD *YES*

There's been a lot of talk about how people are supposed to "say yes to Life" and how that's a winning operating system for a fruitful and meaningful life. The part that's omitted from this statement could be summed up as "*and* say NO to all the bullshit."

Sure, we should say yes to the good things that make life full and rich, but we need to make space for them. We also need to temper these yeses in time. At this buffet of life, we don't need to eat everything in sight in one sitting. Over time, you can feast on what you'd like in between lots of activity and movement, but you need time to digest and assimilate.

Saying yes to something right now more often than not means saying no to something you've already agreed to.

For example, your friends call you up and say, "Let's go for a drink." You impulsively say, "Yes. Okay, great; let's do this!"

You had plans to go to the gym, eat a healthy dinner, and get home to your family. You need to help your son with a project, and it's due next week. But now you've taken down a few drinks, eaten chicken wings and chips, drunk a few more drinks, skipped the workout, and gotten home after the kid went to bed.

That one yes killed three previous yeses. Namely,

Yes to a healthy fitness routine that would boost your energy, clear your head, and make you feel happy in life;

Yes to a healthy dinner that would nourish a robust microbiome, reduce inflammation, feed your cells, hydrate your body, and energize your life; and

Yes to your family that needs you to be a great partner, parent, role model, friend, and positive example of someone who makes the right choices.

Is that one impulsive yes worth backing out of the three yeses you had already committed to? Seldom is *that* answer "Yes."

When we fail to hold the line for something we've already agreed to, we turn the previous yeses into nos with this one new yes. It's like keeping the castle doors open and letting the marauding invaders come and go as they please, hurting our families and robbing us of our health.

Every time we say yes to something, we need to understand that there's an opportunity cost and that there needs to be *time and space* created in our lives for each thing we say yes to.

That's where the Life Garden comes in. When we consciously map out our priorities and commitments, we can use the Life Garden as the screen, or the filter, that allows—or, more importantly, disallows—new "invasive species" to come in and drink from our Water.

It becomes a task of active discernment. Is this friend or foe? Does this add to the Garden, or is it an invasive weed? Where does this fit into my life's plan?

Where will it live in the Life Garden, and where will it draw its Water from?

At what cost?

For every new thing that comes in, we allocate Water (in the form of time, energy, and/or money) for it, whether consciously or unconsciously.

The real question is this: In my current state of limited resources and flickering Vitality, what do I have to give up to take this new thing on?

Is getting drinks with my friends tonight worth skimping on my health and my family? Is it the right use or investment of my life's Water?

The problem is, it's very difficult to make this call at the moment of impulsive reactivity. We are irrational and impulsive beings who are not using our brains and are letting decisions be made for us in life. That seldom works to our benefit. Saying no is a survival skill most of us lack. Is it any wonder we feel spent and unfulfilled?

THE PREFRONTAL CORTEX

The impulsive nature that lies beneath the surface for all of us is tempered by the prefrontal cortex, the area of the brain that can *override* our dumb decisions.

This part of the brain is in charge of the *negation of impulses*.

This is the part of the brain that needs to be active, robust, alert, oxygenated, and full of blood in order to work when we need it. When working correctly, this part of the brain will be actively sitting on its perch and helping us make the right decision at any given moment in time.

When your friends say "Let's go," your impulse may be "Hell yeah, I could use a drink," and without the front of your brain working, you're off on your adventure.

When the prefrontal cortex is engaged, it'll stop you in your tracks and say, "Monkey, no! You said you'd hit the gym, eat well, and get home to help the kid!" which will help you put your foot down for yourself, your life, your better future, and your integrity. You say no to your pals that night and yes to the life you've chosen for yourself. Tragedy averted—you have closed the city gates, and the castle is safe.

THE AMYGDALA

The amygdala is the part of the brain that triggers our "fight or flight" stress response. It helps us get out of nasty situations that can cost us our lives and has helped us instinctively survive.

The problem, though, is that it's always being triggered. We evolved dodging lions and defending our villages. We had to watch for venomous snakes and knew that the smell of smoke meant fire. We developed keen senses for what was truly dangerous and went to "red alert" in those situations. The amygdala is there to help us with that.

Today's world is short-circuiting this system.

Reading a headline about a drone strike in the Middle East, riots in China, a new superbug, volcanic eruptions in Iceland, or an election that swung toward fascism can trigger a response that makes us want to run and hide. In an abstract sense, we're scared for our lives, as the walls seem to be caving in, yet we're sitting in an air-conditioned room on a comfy sofa. Our lives are not usually in immediate danger, yet it feels that way, especially to the amygdala. This primitive circuitry has not evolved as quickly as our technology-driven society.

The danger can be abstract—a psychological fear that is driven by concepts and images but not our immediate reality. This creates a double-edged sword of having a bigger brain with awareness, and the amygdala sensing danger and doing its thing.

The amygdala tells the body to pull resources from higher-order centers of the brain and divert them to the big muscles that'll help us get out of a bad situation. Our body pulls blood away from the front of the brain and toward the hindbrain (or reptilian brain) and diverts it away from the "rest and digest" areas of the gut into the "get me the hell out of here" muscles that are being overtaxed by constant stress.

The amygdala, associated with our *perception* of fear, only knows strife and conflict, and that's where most of us live. In times of stress, it pings the hypothalamus and adjusts hormone and blood sugar levels.[1] We live under the shadow of war, economic collapse, ecological disaster, and the breakdown of civilized society. The amygdala prepares our body for this prolonged war.

Bad things happen in war.

Peacetime is when our humanity shines.

THE SWITCH

In some ways, our nervous system is really quite simple. There are two main states of being that dominate our existence: peacetime and wartime.

The parasympathetic nervous system (PNS) governs our "rest and digest" state of existence. It's the peacetime economy, in which our immune systems are relaxed and doing their jobs, our guts are calm so we can process and digest our foods, we heal our cells, we can rest when tired, we have great sex, and we can make better decisions.

In this state, blood flows to the prefrontal cortex and helps us with discernment and the negation of impulses. It helps us remain rational and think through the consequences of our actions.

This is where we're supposed to live 99 percent of the time. Our ancestors would do their thing, and occasionally, a crisis would either end their lives or leave them alive to enjoy another day. If and when a real emergency was upon them, they'd switch over to the sympathetic nervous system (SNS) and execute emergency powers.

This would trigger all the stuff we spoke about with the amygdala. Blood would divert to the emergency "get me out of here" muscles in our legs to help us flee. It would drain from the front of the brain to the hindbrain, and we'd jack up the hormones cortisol and adrenaline to help squeeze emergency energy out to survive what's meant to be a short, yet extreme, crisis scenario.

Either the lion got you, or it didn't.

Either the midnight raid by the other village killed you, or you fended them off.

Our ancestors really only tapped the sympathetic nervous system a small percentage of the time.[2] That meant most of the time, we lived in a happy, healthy, restful state where we nourished our bodies and made better decisions.

That is not the world we're living in anymore.

We are constantly tapping the SNS and drawing blood away from the front of our brains. We pull resources from our gut and tap our immune system because we see everything as an impending crisis. We get tired, bloated, gassy, moody, and irritated on a daily basis, and we see everyone around us doing the same, and we think it must be normal.

But it is not.

It is killing us and robbing us of the amazing capacity we have to be human.

If we can't access our prefrontal cortex, we are making decisions under duress and are losing our ability to say no to things that don't serve us. It seems like a great decision to get out of immediate pain when you're living in sympathetic dominance, *except it isn't.*

The right decision remains elusive as long as you're living on the wrong side of your neurology.

FLIPPING THE SWITCH

The most important thing you can do to hone your focus and get your life back is to learn how to flip the switch from SNS to PNS dominance.

You can do this consciously and, frankly, it's the key to saving your life.

In my opinion, the only way we can step back into the driver's seat and live our lives mindfully with intention, attention, focus, clarity, and rational insight is to take control of this system and allow our prefrontal cortex to do its job.

What's the job again?

- The negation of impulses
- Higher moral reasoning
- Higher cognitive reasoning
- And more . . .

Here's an excerpt from the *International Encyclopedia of the Social & Behavioral Sciences* (italics are my emphasis):[3]

> The prefrontal cortex is profusely connected with many other parts of the brain, notably limbic formations and cortical regions of the parietal and temporal lobes. It has two major anatomical and functional subdivisions: the orbitomedial and the dorsolateral prefrontal regions. The orbitomedial cortex is involved in sensory processing (taste and olfaction), *regulation of the internal environment, control of drives,*

and emotional behavior. The dorsolateral cortex is involved in cognitive functions. The prefrontal cortex as a whole plays a cardinal role in the temporal organization of behavior and cognitive activities. *It controls the execution, order and timing of sequential acts toward a goal.* The dorsolateral prefrontal cortex, in particular, is essential for the *planning and execution of complex new temporal structures of behavior, speech and logical reasoning.* Two cognitive functions of temporal integration mediate the organization of these activities: short-term memory and preparatory set. The dorsolateral prefrontal cortex supports both these functions in cooperation with other cortical and subcortical structures.

All the stuff we've been talking about—curating your life, making better decisions, allowing room for your dreams, and nourishing focus, intent, and clarity—hinges on your being able to maintain the ability to hold the line. The prefrontal cortex helps us control our impulsive drives ("I'll get a drink with my friends") and execute sequential acts toward a goal ("I'm going to get healthy and get my life together").

You know what else suppresses the prefrontal cortex? Alcohol. We're all stumbling around like drunk idiots making too many bad decisions.

Okay, cool. I get it . . . so how do we flip the switch?

The answer is so simple it's embarrassing, and you're not going to like it.

It's advice you may have heard and ignored before.

Meditation and mind-body practices are the safest and most effective ways to trigger PNS dominance and shift us toward a more mindful and deliberate mindset. Deep, lower diaphragmatic breathing and mindful movement trigger PNS dominance. That's what meditation and yoga, Tai Chi, Qigong, and other internal practices start with.

So I breathe to my lower belly, and I'm done?

No, that's a start. Note the word *start*. The key is to develop a practice where you *keep doing it*. We need to start swinging the pendulum back. We've spent our entire lives getting dragged into stress, strife, and conflict, and our nervous systems are accustomed to the shitshow.

We need to start working our way back into the driver's seat. That means daily practice.[4,5]

It is 100 percent true.

The catch that you won't like is this: *you* have to do it yourself.

Nobody can do this for you. You can't flop on a table and say "fix me" to some guru or doctor. It's a personal practice that takes effort and where the yields are hundredfold. There's no solution, book, or person out there that's going to "fix" you with shortcuts.

You have to fix yourself.

LENGTHENING THE FUSE

I've known lots of patients over the years that claimed meditation didn't work for them because they tried it in the middle of a panic attack and it didn't stop the angst.

By then it's too late.

We need to do meditation and mind-body practice every single day in order to *not go there*.

We need to constantly train the nervous system to shift back to the PNS so we can live in a state of "rest and digest" peacefulness to lengthen our fuse for when things get hectic.

These practices are not designed as some spiritual ripcord that we pull once the madness has already taken us over; that's just silly. It's a mark of how idiotic our culture has become—pop a chill pill and get back to being a crazed person. That's not the way. The more we meditate, the less likely we are to get agitated. The more we learn to live in this state, the less we get knocked off our perch. If we do lose our cool, we come back to center faster.

Meditation builds resilience—both psychological and neurological. It helps the brain adapt to changing stimuli, and it helps us manage stress in our lives.

What does this have to do with focus?

Everything.

You are the problem. Your reactivity and amygdala-driven emotional survival state are driving the impulsive decisions that keep you from getting the life you want. If you can't hold the line for yourself, you're doomed to a life drifting out to sea and getting pushed around by the competing forces trying to blow you around. That's the *opposite* of focus.

The only way to avoid that is to set a course and stick to it with meticulous, diligent focus and intent.

This means saying no when someone says, "Oh, look at that island there. Let's go there!" Plotting your course means saying no to the myriad other destinations that tempt you.

It doesn't mean you can't be adaptive, but it certainly means you keep your head straight and make conscious decisions in your life.

A master of life has mastered their impulses.

That's where meditation and mind-body practice excel. They've been around for thousands of years and are the safest and most compelling things we can do to get hold of ourselves, switch back to parasympathetic dominance, activate our prefrontal cortex, and, frankly, stand a chance of truly living life in this distraction-ridden world.

The ancient sages and the brain scientists have come together on this in recent years.

What the ancients deemed the "third eye" is exactly where the prefrontal cortex sits in our forehead. The higher spiritual awakening and the functions we gain from calming the mind and focusing our attention to this part of the brain have remarkable similarities. To master life, we need control of this part of our brain and consciousness. It's all the same thing—just different languages trying to explain it over the millennia.

I've created a number of free meditation resources for you that can be downloaded at theurbanmonk.com/focus. For now, know that it's not optional. You need to be doing something daily to offset the insidious pull away from your higher cognitive functions.

WEEDING YOUR GARDEN

The Life Garden then becomes a powerful tool, filter, and operating system to help you process new information coming in and radically transform your life—*if you show up* and do your part. The mind-body practices will train you to get focused and stay focused. Without focus, this'll be yet another start/stop thing that you failed. Once you do that, you'll have proven to yourself that failing is what you do, which makes it easier to do it again.

That cycle needs to stop with you.

You need to stop it by waking up to the present moment and then keep coming back to it again and again. As time slides past us, we fall into distraction. Coming back to the present moment is a relentless pursuit, not some satori flash with a glittery explosion that happens and then we're done. That's a misread of scripture and a neo-Zen BS fairy tale. We need to work at staying aware and awake—always.

Get the Marvel comics and superhero stuff out of your head. The "special powers" that really matter are the ones closest to home—the ability to maintain equanimity and to be the eye in the center of the storm.

A calm, collected human who has focus and intent fused together is a force of nature.

This person can plant things and see them manifest in short order in their life—that is, once the field is clear and the soil is fertile.

That said, now we look to weeding our Garden.

Go back to the work you did in Chapter 2, and let's examine it. What are the biggest plants or items in each of the areas of Health, Career, Family and Friends, Life's Passions, and Desired Things in your life?

Now let's dive into each category and start to think about the possible weeds in each of these areas. Weeds are hard to identify because we are good at kidding ourselves. We justify and rationalize everything, or else we'd feel like complete idiots.

A weed pulls Water—in the form of time, energy, or money—from your life, even though you have not identified it as an important plant in your Life Garden. It could be a TV show, a toxic person, some aspect of your business that loses money and causes all the stress, or maybe even an addiction.

Do you play sudoku for 40 minutes a day and call it "downtime"? Good, then we've found what could be your meditation time instead! Nothing is inherently wrong with sudoku, but if it's taking time away from your stated goals, then it's a weed right now.

On your drive home, are you making random calls to people who don't fill your life? Now we've found your time to listen to books that'll water your passion or career.

It could also be a negative meme or toxic belief that no longer serves you. A lot of us have negative self-worth issues that were passed down from our parents. Or there may be unspoken beliefs around money, love, marriage, politics, race, or whatever else that we have picked up and embedded in the fertile soil of our subconscious minds. These can be influencing our decisions and impacting the positive trajectory of our lives. Weeds!

Look around for where your Water is leaking. There will always be something mooching off it. It'll oftentimes feel familiar and safe, having nestled in there long ago.

If it isn't a plant you've identified in your Life Garden, then it's a weed.

If you disagree, then make it a plant and make room for it in your Garden. You get to choose, but you have to be accountable to yourself. If you make it a plant, you'll need to budget Water to it. That's fine, but answer these questions first:

> What do you have to pull Water away from to feed this thing?
> What are you needing to say no to in order to keep this thing a yes?

If mastery is in the negation, we need to leave room in our lives for the things we choose to honor and value.

We have to hold this space over time and not get distracted. It's very easy to make a plan and stick to it for a few days, maybe even weeks. But what about months from now? Doing big, meaningful things may sometimes take years of dedication and focus.

My wife and I have some friends that just came out of three years of severe austerity trying to get out of debt. Some people mocked them for not coming out to dinner and missing life events, but now they're debt-free, and their stress levels have dropped significantly.

It took *three years* of dedication and focus.

Now let's go through your items from your Chapter 2 homework and identify the weeds in each area of your Garden. Also, are there any weeds living in between the various areas? Spend some time really delving into this. Go for a few walks, and let things percolate.

Here's the thing about weeds:

They hide.

They disguise themselves as plants.

They lie low when you look for them.

Because life is about survival. Everything wants to continue to live—even ideas.

Remember, the Qi follows the Shen.

Energy follows thought. So if you had an idea about something a few years ago and you put some time and energy into it, it has life. You breathed life into that idea. Now several years have passed and nothing has come of it. Perhaps it needs a fresh breath of air or some CPR. Okay, that's cool. Add it to your Garden. But what if its time has passed? Then it's time to identify it as a weed and stop watering it.

Better yet, let's do a weed-cutting ceremony. When you identify something as a weed, close your eyes and think about it. Go back to the original moment it came into your life—the introduction, the idea, the inception. See it. Thank it for coming into your life, and then tell it you no longer need it. In your mind, visualize it as a weed and pull it up from the soil of your Life Garden.

Now, here is a really important step: take the weed and bury it back in the soil of your Life Garden. Thank it for its service, and assure it that it will be laid to rest to act as mulch for the future life that will grow in its stead. See it getting absorbed into the soil of your Life Garden and *feeding* the plants you've put there intentionally. This will be a willful and conscious transfer of energy that will honor your past ideas and energies. It will help you let go of the old ideas and people who served you in the past but no longer do so in the present. It's okay. Let them go.

This is the cycle of life.

BETTER BOUNDARIES

Boundaries suck. Most people are people pleasers, so the thought of letting someone down is painful.

From our parents, siblings, friends, co-workers, to even the random guy at the store, we want people to like us.

It's so hard for us to say no to people because we don't want to look like jerks. We fear that taking a stand for ourselves comes across as selfish.

"What do you mean you won't come to the movies with us? Are you too good for your high school buddies now?"

"Actually, I've got to get to bed early because I have a big meeting tomorrow that can really boost my career. Nothing personal, but I need to take care of my family."

It's hard to do. It's hard with people, and it's hard with time.

"I feel guilty taking 45 minutes to work out each day because I should be spending that time with my aging mom."

So now you have no energy to tend to your own life, let alone your mom's health.

Ringing a bell?

We all do it.

Culturally, we've bound ourselves to each other in a complicated web of co-dependencies. Here are just a few examples:

I take care of you financially, and you help me emotionally.

I ignore your anger, and you ignore my pill popping.

I listen to your complaints, and you invite me into your social circle.

I watch movies with you when you're lonely, and you make home-cooked meals.

The list goes on and on. Not all of it is insidious, but that's why it gets complicated.

Mom is sweet, kind, cooks hot meals, and is there to watch the grandchildren, but she's also sharp in her criticism of your parenting and offers unsolicited life and marriage advice every chance she gets.

Dad helps you tinker with the tools in the garage, and you enjoy talking about sports with him, but he's also a drunk asshole who's verbally abusive to his new wife.

Do you ignore it? We've gotten buried in our tacit deals—the unspoken contracts with the people in our lives.

When's the last time you've evaluated the costs of these deals?

This is part of your work as we identify the weeds in your Garden. What spoken or unspoken agreements do you have with friends, family, co-workers, or lovers that need to be looked at through an honest lens?

News flash: this is where you're going to identify lots of leaking Water—the very Water you've complained about not having and that you need to nourish the plants you really want in your Garden to give you the life you choose.

The degree to which you are honest with yourself will directly correlate with the success you achieve in doing this work. It requires radical honesty—not with me but with yourself.

THE SCIENCE OF HABITS

How you got into your current situation is a result of the thousands of little habits you picked up along the way. In high school, perhaps you were on the track team and would come home to a bag of chips and some dip. That worked fine for an 18-year-old kid with a raging metabolism, but now you're 40, and you kept the habit and forgot to adjust your "burn rate."

Maybe you grew up earning your dessert for good deeds around the house, and now sugar is the thing you identify as a treat for yourself.

The list goes on and on because we're essentially creatures of habit. In neurology, the saying is "Neurons that fire together wire together."

This deserves a moment here.

Up until a couple of decades ago, the common belief in neurology was that once we get to a certain "height" of brain development, then it is downhill from there. Now we understand that there's this thing called "neuroplasticity," which means new neuronal pathways can be laid down and enhanced well into our adult lives.

And if neurons that fire together wire together, then this discovery is huge.

If we make a habit of checking social media every time we have a "moment to relax," then our neurons will keep wiring into a habit that becomes an addiction. Now we are "that person" who can't look away from our phone every chance we get, whether it's the itch to see what's new or whatever other reason we plug into that world.

By the same token, and this is a key point here, if we cue ourselves to take 10 deep breaths and relax every time we're put on hold, hit a red light, or have a timer go off on our phones, we can equally train the neurons in our brain to do something magical. We can wire our brain to truly relax and go into an *alpha wave* brain state at will. We can train ourselves to "flip the switch" to parasympathetic nervous system dominance and wire our brains to become more relaxed, resilient, and capable of making better decisions.

We are the sum total of all the habits (good and bad) that we've picked up on this journey of life. We have thousands of little microhabits that go mostly unnoticed and unquestioned that are part of our daily, weekly, and monthly routines. And these are some of the juicy weeds we need to dig up.

This is a great opportunity to examine your life and see where you may be doing things that don't serve you anymore. Perhaps you used to smoke when you drank and now you smoke during work breaks, giving you bad breath, stinky fingers, and possible lung cancer.

Maybe you were forced to finish your plate as a kid, and now you simply don't stop eating until it's all gone.

Does this still serve you?

If the answer to any of the questions you think of is no, then it's time to program new habits. New habits take over 90 days to really settle in, so you'll need to be patient with this process. If you know it takes a while and commit to it, it makes it easier to suck it up and keep moving in the right direction.

You will wire new habits and lay down new neuronal pathways. You will water the plants you choose to grow versus the weeds you've grown accustomed to seeing.

This may look like taking a walk alone or with a friend during work breaks instead of hanging with the smoker crew. It may mean doing therapy and tantra courses with your spouse and finding true intimacy in your relationship. It may mean dishing smaller portions onto your plate.

There are dozens of these little switches that will need to be flipped in order for you to get a handle on your Garden. Water is leaking left and right. You have to find the leaks and redirect the Water to helpful and healthy places into the light of your intentionally curated Life Garden.

ROME WASN'T BUILT IN A DAY

It'll take a while to get this right.

It takes 90–100 days to really imprint a new habit, and that's why we're going to help you map out your Life Garden and then take actionable steps in 100-day sprints to start seeing some lasting changes in your life. One hundred days may seem long, but guess what? Whether you do the work or not, 100 days from now, you'll be 100 days older, and you'll have either reinforced old habits (watered your weeds) or laid the foundation for new and healthier habits (uprooted the weeds and cleaned up the flow of Water).

What's it going to be?

The right decision is to start rewiring these neurons right now and never look back.

Plotting your life's course in 100-day sprints makes change manageable and less daunting. A 10-year plan is cute, but the steps that you need to take to get there may not be as realistically plottable.

That's why we're going to get even more granular. You will make one- and five-year plans and then work backward so you can map out the necessary steps to get yourself there. We're going to have 30-, 60-, and 100-day plans for each "Gong" you do. Remember, the word *Gong* in Chinese means "work."

This is your work.

The translation of *Gong Fu* (or "kung fu") is "hard work." Life is hard work, whether you're driving or being driven. When you're back on your heels, life is rough, and you limp away bruised. When you get better at life, your Gong Fu is good. It means you can tackle bigger problems and fight tougher opponents.

As we engage in our Gongs, we move closer and closer to a life we choose. We pull the weeds, trim the hedges, and get more and more intentional with where our Water goes. This brings increased focus.

Over time, we start to prove to ourselves that we can win. We deliver proof to our psyche that we are capable of positive change and laying new habits to supplant old ones. We create a positive and constructive place where we can channel our Vitality. We see our plants thrive in our Life Garden and we get better at identifying weeds, even the trickiest ones.

Some of us start with weeds that have sprouted to towering heights. We need to cut the Water and slowly move resources away from these.

This process is about getting real, being real, and staying real with yourself. Society often pulls us in the opposite direction, so it'll feel awkward at first. Honesty is awkward. It can be uncomfortable and sometimes feels yucky.

That's certainly better than continuing one more day of lying to yourself and watering the weeds that strip you of your very life force.

In Chapter 8, we'll discuss some more advanced Life Gardening principles like identifying weeds and redirecting Water. Again, life is messy, and we need to allow for some wiggle room to handle the complexity. There's also a boatload of emotional trauma we're all carrying around, so allowing time and space to heal and deal with it becomes critical as we grow.

But for now, we need to get you some wins and build you up so you have the power, energy, agency, and clarity to look backward and dig.

Let's calm your mind and reduce your stress. Let's boost your Vitality and get you more energy for your day-to-day.

From there, we will build on it and continue to heal and grow. Rome wasn't built in a day, but better habits are best started *right now*. The sooner we start, the sooner you'll feel better and be able to invest your newfound energy in further growth.

In the next chapter, I'll give you a shot in the arm and help you get into the work with some added energy and Vitality.

LIFE GARDENING HOMEWORK

LOOKING FOR WEEDS

Go back to the work you did at the end of Chapter 2, and let's examine it.

What are the biggest plants or items in each of the areas in your Life Garden—Health, Career, Family and Friends, Life's Passions, and Desired Things? List them out here.

The Most Important Plants in My Life Garden (from Chapter 2)

Health
Career
Family and Friends
Life's Passions
Desired Things

Now go through your items from Chapter 2 and see if you can identify weeds in each area.

Are you able to detect any weeds in this list? Knowing what you know now, look deeper and really question what may have snuck in under your radar. List them below.

The Weeds I Can Identify in Each Area of My Garden

> *Health*
> *Career*
> *Family and Friends*
> *Life's Passions*
> *Desired Things*

BOUNDARIES

What spoken or unspoken agreements do you have with friends, family, co-workers, or lovers that need to be looked at through an honest lens? This is where poor boundaries come in and crush our own lives, dreams, and aspirations. Please jot down all the breaches in boundaries that may be affecting each area of your Life Garden.

Places in My Life Garden Where Poor Boundaries May Be Impacting Me

> *Health*
> *Career*
> *Family and Friends*
> *Life's Passions*
> *Desired Things*

TOXIC MEMES

Let's revisit the Subconscious Programming from Chapter 3. We've discussed the mental viruses that may be getting in our way. Let's dive deeper and see if we can identify more of them.

> What subconscious beliefs are getting in my way?
> What viral memes can I identify that are driving my personality?
> What core beliefs stand between me and a brighter future?
> If I'm having trouble finding weeds, where may they be hiding in plain sight?

WEED-CUTTING CEREMONY

Here are the steps for a mental ceremony I'd like you to try with weeds you find, whether they are behaviors or beliefs.

When you identify something as a weed, close your eyes and think about it.

Go back to the original moment it came into your life— the introduction, the idea, the inception.

See it.

Thank it for coming into your life, and then tell it you no longer need it.

In your mind, see it as a weed, and pull it up from the soil of your Life Garden.

If you're not ready to let it go, then find a place in your Garden for it—that's fine. If you decide there's simply no room for it, then it's time to let it go.

Take the weed, and bury it back in the soil of your Life Garden.

Thank it for its service, and assure it that it will be laid to rest to act as mulch for future life that will grow in its stead.

CHAPTER SIX

BRINGING UP YOUR POWER

Most people don't know what to do with the energy in a lump of coal, let alone a tank of jet fuel. There's raw power trapped in both that can be released. Without an engineered direction, setting fuel on fire generates an *explosion*. That's not the chaos we want in life.

What we want with that fuel is *propulsion* so that our rocket blasts off to a specific destination.

It turns out we all need to be rocket scientists in our own lives. We need to think. That means we'll need our brains to work.

Going back to our Life Garden, we need to create a system that takes Water and injects it into very specific areas where it can fuel us in a *desired* direction.

We can open up the tap once we know there are no leaks in the system.

MORE ENERGY = MORE WATER

Straight up, more energy equals more Water for your Garden. It'll help get resources to all your plants and fuel your dreams. That's why energy drinks are so popular. Who wouldn't want more energy?

But that's fake energy.

It's not okay borrowing from tomorrow's energy to get through today. This insane deficit spending model is killing us. It grinds our cells, taxes our adrenals and our immunity, and keeps us in a "fight or flight" operating system that doesn't allow us to relax. No wonder we feel so time compressed.

Let's talk about *real energy*.

Think of a power plant. It takes fuel in the form of coal, gasoline, or nuclear materials, unleashes the energy trapped in that fuel, and spins out the electrons coming from those reactions through turbines that generate energy and send it down the power line.

Once that energy is recovered from the thing that is burning or reacting, it flies out of the power plant and *needs to be used*.

If people aren't using power at that hour, the power plant slows down or shuts off. There's no point in wasting resources that we are not using. Our battery technology isn't good enough yet, so we can't really store energy in our power grid effectively.

The cutting edge of technology right now is in solving this problem. Our batteries are getting better, but they're big, clunky, and filled with toxic metals that don't recycle well.

In California, one way the power plants have been handling this issue is that they use the excess energy output at night to pump huge volumes of water back up a hill so it can run back down the turbines of a dam during the day and generate more energy when it's actually needed. That's a nice work-around, but it doesn't solve the energy storage problem.

So how does nature solve this problem?

Fat.

Our bodies use fat to store energy.

It's big, fluffy, and clunky, and we don't like looking at it, but boy can it store energy. In fact, most of us have more energy in storage than we'd like, *yet we feel tired.* We don't know how to access it and hate that it's there.

Adenosine triphosphate (ATP) plays a central role in this saga. It's a carrier molecule that essentially allows for the transfer of energy from our food to our cells. Without getting too deep into the mechanics of it all (it's complicated), the body takes sugars, proteins, and fats and has different pathways to break them down. Each has a slightly different result, but taken together, they provide a broad array of areas we can draw energy from to run our lives.

The citric acid cycle (CAC), aka the Krebs cycle or TCA cycle (tricarboxylic acid cycle), is a complex system of chemical reactions that happen inside our mitochondria where carbohydrates, proteins, and fats are stripped of the energy stored in their bonds. This energy needs a place to live, and that's where ATP comes in. Consider ATP the body's universal energy currency, a molecule that's essentially accepted everywhere. Our cells can take the energy stored in the ATP and fuel the metabolic processes that allow this thing we call *life.*

There are many nuances to how this happens with different macromolecules, but for our purposes, know that energy comes from these macromolecules (carbs, proteins, and fats) and *is either used or stored.*

Fat carries the highest density of energy of all macromolecules. It's nature's storage device for energy, so when we don't need it, we're storing it. Even if the energy came from carbs we just ate, if we have more than we need, our body will create fat to store the excess.

In order to use this energy, your muscles have to call for it. Your brain needs to demand it. In short, you have to increase the legitimate demand to make sure this stored energy gets where it's needed.

THE MITOCHONDRIA

All ATP formation happens in the mitochondria, the tiny little organelles that live in the nucleus of each cell. They help strip energy from foods and kick out ATP. These tiny organelles came from an ancient form of bacteria that joined together with our cells to create nature's best example of symbiosis. They play a central role in the powering up of our lives.

It stands to reason that we like these guys.

In fact, we want them to be bigger, healthier, and happier, and we want more of them.

And that all happens when we add lean muscle mass.

The big muscles in your body (including the heart muscle) have the highest density of mitochondria. This means as you improve your cardio fitness, your heart will have more mitochondria to call upon. Your legs, glutes, thighs, and other big muscles are huge in this. That's why squats, deadlifts, box jumps, and leg presses help build up your power. Even taking hikes and climbing stairs contributes to this. These exercises bring more mitochondria to the party.

As we up the number of mitochondria and boost their capacity, we have more places where we can turn food into energy. We increase our metabolic rate and burn more calories at rest. We also burn more calories when we do all that exercise, adding demand for fuel in your body. Your food feeds healthy places where positive growth is happening, namely muscle mass that's metabolically active.

CALORIES IN

Building up the fire is a solid plan, but it takes a while. You can also cut the fuel coming in. This is less fun but super effective. When the power plant has reduced demand, the natural reaction is to stop adding fuel to the fire. For a number of reasons, it's harder for us to do that with our bodies. This has to do with levels of leptin and ghrelin, two hormones that signal for satiety levels, in the brain. These are easily manipulated by levels of toxins in our foods, insulin, stress, and sleep. Essentially, the chemical messengers that are there to tell us to stop eating are on the fritz. Eating clean, natural foods and cutting sugars will help fix this, as will the recommendations at the end of this chapter.

However, one of the most effective ways of addressing the issue is cutting calories so that you burn more of your excess stored fuel.

If you take on less fuel, you won't need to store it in the form of fat and will eventually burn off the fat you have.

In my experience, living life fully means having a healthy appetite because you're charging all day. If you eat according to the recommendations in Chapter 4, you'll be getting lots of phytonutrients, fiber, water, and minerals without too many calories.

Eat lots of low-glycemic vegetables and keep going; it's good for your microbiome and colon health anyhow. You can increase your burn rate with exercise and see how your appetite changes. You'll likely be hungry more often.

It's really pretty simple. The body needs to move, so get moving. Keep making adjustments to the calories you take in so you feel great and burn off the excess fat and feel healthy.

EXCESS FAT IS POTENTIAL ENERGY

Let's judo flip the "I hate my body" crap that runs through our heads.

You've been looking for energy . . .

It's right there. Look in the mirror.

Cool. Check. I see it.

Now let's unlock it and kill two birds with one stone.

Burning fat happens when we exercise. A moderately elevated heart rate on a 90-minute power walk or hike will put us in a fat-burning zone. So will high-intensity interval training (HIIT), if you can handle it right now.

Essentially, moving the body, getting fit, breathing fresh air, sweating, and getting stronger are the way out. Don't let all the fad diet noise fool you; get out and move.

Then *keep moving.*

Motion begets more motion. Soon you'll be feeling better, and you'll never look back.

KETOSIS

Ketosis occurs when the body isn't getting enough carbs to run on the "easy economy," so it has to start burning fat. In nature, there's hardly any fat in the foods we eat. We make it and store it for a rainy day—the emergency energy fund. But our unhealthy foods and engineered diets have ruined that now. We get too much fat coming at us, and we store the excess—lots of excess.

The problem?

Our bodies don't want to let it go.

This stuff is precious in case there's a famine. We live in "fight or flight," and that signals our bodies to store the fat.

That's why it's so hard to lose. That's why one strategy is to force the body's hand.

If all you eat for a prolonged period of time is healthy fats and proteins, the body has no choice but to start using them as fuel. When the stomach is empty, it'll scavenge elsewhere for it. Ideally, it will pull the fat from your excess storage and burn that versus tearing down muscle tissue.

Muscle is precious.

It's the most valuable type of tissue that helps us be strong and robust, and it carries most of our mitochondria. When we lose muscle, it helps us lose weight, but the net effect is loss, where we are taking a step backward. It slows the energy-producing capacity of the body.

The key to ketosis is to burn fat, eat plenty of protein, and avoid breaking down our muscles, keeping our power plant humming.

In my opinion, this works well if you have a lot of weight you'd like to lose, but in the long run, carbs are your friend. I've found that for sustained energy and longevity, the best diets will use keto principles to maximize fat metabolism while still delivering plenty of healthy vegetables, fruits, nuts, seeds, and lean proteins to the body. Some call this "Paleo," but that word has been bastardized by now.

Eat stuff that comes from the earth, without any enhance-ment, modifications, processing, or whatever else we often do to it.

An apple is food. Apple juice is not.

Celery is awesome. Celery crackers sound gross.

An elk out in the wild has eaten natural grasses all its life; the cow you're eating has had forests cleared for its grazing and was likely fed corn and soy and pumped full of hormones to pull in more money per pound.

Eat real food.

Eat plants, not junk made in processing plants.

In addition, subtle adjustments in burn rate can help you to burn energy more effectively. Here are my favorites.

Time-Restricted Feeding

This is when you elect to tighten your eating window to just a few hours. The typical one that's turned heads in a handful of new studies shows that a 16/8 cycle (16 hours fasting followed by an 8-hour eating window) helps drop weight and improve insulin resistance (which counters diabetes and adjusts leptin and ghrelin levels).[6] This means that you eat in an 8-hour window and refrain from taking in any calories in the other 16. For me, I stop eating at 7 P.M. and eat my first meal at 11 A.M. I do this because dinner time is family time, and I'd rather eat with them. Others flip it. It doesn't matter as long as you keep your eating window under 8 hours.

Now, some like to extend that. I have colleagues that only eat one meal a day and keep to a 4-hour window. That works for them. You need to see what works for you.

The first few days of this can be tough, but you get used to it quickly, and then it's amazing. Your body isn't screaming and freaking out when there's no sugar to burn. Instead, it quietly goes and finds some stored fat in your belly or hips and uses that instead. Your mood starts to stabilize, and that "hangry" person starts to chill out, and you build resilience over time.

Of all the strategies for diet, this is my favorite one.

In the eight-hour eating window, I like to eat lean, healthy meats, lots of vegetables, and low-glycemic fruits, nuts, and seeds. I also drink plenty of water. I do not then take down ice cream at 11:01 A.M. Use this window to get a handle on your satiety and feed your body good fuel. You're essentially limiting your caloric intake and giving your body more time to heal while fasting.

Intermittent Fasting

While some people use the term "intermittent fasting" to describe the time-restricted feeding strategy detailed above, a more accurate definition is fasting for longer periods of time at random intervals. It helps trick the body into thinking your diet is unpredictable and can't be trusted, so it needs to burn fat. People using this strategy will often fast, drinking only water, for two to three days a week and mix it up. Three to five days of water fasting here and there can be tremendously therapeutic, but it's not easy.

This strategy works well for people who have relatively healthy adrenals and are not diabetic or prediabetic. *Please please please* don't be a monkey. Work with a qualified physician on this, and make sure they know what they're doing. The Institute for Functional Medicine is a great place to find a good doctor.

Water Fasting

Fasting is rough, particularly fasting on only water. It makes you feel tired, cranky, faint, and a whole host of other unpleasant things. That said, it can be great for you. A typical water fast can last three to five days with only water and some salt here and there to keep your electrolytes in balance. I don't recommend doing prolonged water fasting without a good doctor on board, particularly since many people have hypoglycemia and are prediabetic.

Overall, we're so damned stressed out that we often can't take major stressors like fasting too well.

After all, fasting is actual starvation, which the body doesn't usually think is very cool.

However, it kicks our survivor genes into high gear and gets us to adapt better. Our body will burn fat. It'll scavenge for and break down food wherever it can, and—this is the kicker—it'll pull weak, dead, or unneeded tissue off first.

That means we heal.

Fasting can help the body heal.

It can help normalize blood sugar (again, work with a doctor).

It can kick us into ketosis and help us get better at burning fat.

It's a good strategy when we need to take a break and reset our body.

All this said, I still recommend time-restricted feeding for most patients at the start. It helps shift the body to burn fat and is less disruptive to daily life. You still need to think, move, drive, and basically function every day.

I'm a firm believer that the path to wellness needs to be doable or people simply won't do it. That's counterproductive and a waste of time.

Rome wasn't built in a day. You can do this. Start today.

BACK TO OUR ENERGY ECONOMICS

The essence of having and maintaining healthy Energy Economics is very similar to basic accounting. You want to increase the assets and cash flow while minimizing the liabilities. That way your balance sheet looks good and you're deemed creditworthy and solvent.

In terms of the energy flow of our life, it's all about boosting our body's ability to efficiently extract energy from food and use it in the right ways. This means adding lean muscle mass and powering the brain. Of course, there are also the daily operations. We need energy for digestion, immunity, excretion, hormone synthesis, and a whole host of other day-to-day operations that keep us alive. All of these are vitally important, and all of them require energy.

The key is to attain efficiency in each area. Let's take digestion and excretion, for instance.

We've already looked at gut function and digestion a couple of times. This is where food is broken down, absorbed, assimilated, and excreted through a complex series of processes involving saliva, proper chewing, enzymes, hydrochloric acid, a healthy colony of helpful symbiotic bacteria, the gut-associated lymphatic tissue (GALT), carrier proteins, mitochondria, the urinary bladder, the gallbladder, the liver, the small and large intestines, and much, much more.

At each step, there's energy needed and burned, and there are so many places where we can optimize efficiency and *save energy*. In fact, the better we get at it, the more energy we can properly extract from our food.

Let's call that profit.

In regard to excretion, say you don't eat enough fiber and are dehydrated. Your body has to work overtime to try to push the toxins out, taxing your liver and your colon. The backed-up toxins then wreak havoc on the body, and the immune system has to get involved. Now you're tired and can't think clearly and don't get the deal you've been working on at the office. Now money is tight, and you have to cancel your gym membership. Just keep following this thread down in any example in your own life.

Optimizing our lifestyle for peak efficiency helps us extract more energy to live our lives fully. We want to cut the expenses as best we can.

The habit of having a bottle of wine in the evening and then watching TV for a couple of hours to decompress is an extremely inefficient way to manage stress.

The wine jacks up your blood sugar and acts as a mild stimulant, which pushes your sleep time back a few hours. Even when you do sleep, your liver is now working to conjugate and detox the alcohol out of your body. You toss, turn, sweat, wake up to drink water, wake back up to pee, and basically cut your sleep quality in half on a nightly basis. Then the next day you can't function without that first cup of coffee and are filling the second cup before getting in your car. You struggle through work, make some mistakes, miss the gym, and swear to yourself you'll get back in there next week.

Perhaps a better form of nightcap is in order?

Another serious expense to our body is junk food. This makes your gut work overtime, and then your liver has to pick up the slack to help get all those chemicals out of your body. It's a waste of energy that makes your brain numb and stores excess fat where you don't want it. Junk food feeds the wrong kinds of bacteria, which produce substances (lipopolysaccharides) that cause inflammation and disease, versus the good bacteria that help produce more ATP—along with beneficial hormones, butyrate, and vitamins—in the gut. In fact, lots of our B vitamins are synthesized by beneficial bacteria in our guts. Doesn't it make sense to feed and care for them?

THE WHEEL OF VITALITY

Good Energy Economics really comes down to managing the overall Vitality better. This means having a diet, exercise, sleep, and mindset that are healthy and in balance. As each area of your life begins to get better, there will be more energy available to you. You'll get more clarity, enthusiasm, optimism, and power to drive your thoughts and make them a reality.

That's the work we're doing here. You'll need energy to work through the problems that are in your way.

That means getting serious about cutting liabilities and reducing expenses. Only you can do that in your life. You'll need to look around and be honest with yourself.

Where am I being dumb?

Where am I insisting on keeping a behavior that doesn't serve me?

I've had this argument with dozens of people in the clinic when we come up against something that's obviously a problem.

Common example: the nightly ritual is to eat cheese on bread with wine to decompress.

Problem: they are allergic to dairy, but they say, "I'll never part with my cheese. I love it more than life." This is actually a result of the impartial breakdown of cheese. Part of it is from digestive insufficiency, and another part is from harboring the wrong gut bacteria. The resulting molecules include casomorphin, which is a morphine-like derivative that makes people addicted to cheese.

Letting go of opium isn't fun, but it is the right move.

Here's the challenge I see all too often: people have no healthy ritual built in to take off the edge. They have no stress-management routine and zero skills to help calm their nervous systems. They are medicating the best way they can to feel calm and less edgy.

I get it.

The answer is to self-medicate with something that doesn't have terrible side effects. Yes, cutting off your head will solve your migraine problem, but there must be a better way.

And there is.

It's called meditation, and it's been around for millennia.

MIND-BODY PRACTICES

Since the beginning of time, people have been doing mind-body practices. They are woven into the fabric of our history and have been a major part of our religions, cultures, and daily routines. Yoga is ancient and powerful. It has helped billions of people. So has Tai Chi.

Billions of people over the millennia have done this stuff. Tens of thousands of people do Tai Chi and Qigong every day in China. These are very pragmatic people. No one has time or energy to waste, yet they take the time to do this work daily.

There's a reason: *it works*.

Mind-body practices help calm the nerves, reduce systemic inflammation (by modulating the gene expression of NF-κB),[7] bring us back to PNS dominance, facilitate blood and lymph flow, strengthen leg and postural muscles, detox the body, prevent injuries, reduce blood pressure, boost immunity, and much more.

This list goes on and on. Pretty much every major ailment that's wrecking society can be helped with these practices.

Let's take a closer look at a few of these modalities.

Yoga

The ancient practice of *yoga* means "union," as in "union with the Divine." The original forms of yoga mostly involve deep abdominal breathing and the use of certain postures that mimic the Sanskrit alphabet. Early practitioners used these postures and altered states to communicate with the Divine and transform the material essence of their bodies into a lighter vibration. The essential work of creating the "light body" was alive and well in these early traditions.

Toward the late 1800s, much of the practice we know today was being hatched. The British colonists took interest in these practices, and the early forms of modern yoga were created as a hybrid of dynamic postures with modern calisthenics.

Interestingly, the early schools of yoga were predominantly for young men in military training. The "warrior pose" was just that. It helped channel these young men's energy into productive areas while keeping them off the streets.

Today, millions of people swear by yoga and practice it daily. It's an incredible way to relax the body, anchor the breath, calm the mind, and find peace without the cheesecake and wine.

Qigong

Qigong (pronounced "chee gong") mind-body practices originated in Asia and have been around for millennia. It consists of slow, deliberate movement with the coordination of your eyes, mind, body, and breath. There are various forms that come from the martial arts, the health arts, and the temple lineages.

China, Japan, Korea, Thailand, Vietnam, Sri Lanka, and pretty much every other culture in Asia have Qigong traditions.

Personally, I find Qigong to be the most effective way to capture my monkey mind and anchor my consciousness firmly in my body. I've learned hundreds of different sets from various teachers and feel like there's something for everyone in this type of practice. This is my drug of choice.

Tai Chi

Lots of Westerners know of Tai Chi. It's what you see senior people doing in the park. It looks very much like Qigong because it's anchored in Qigong breathing. However, Tai Chi is a branch of kung fu, with the movements practiced very slowly and gracefully. It is tremendous for balance, coordination, and circulation. It's very relaxing and helps build strong leg muscles (which are filled with fresh, strong mitochondria).

Tai Chi is an excellent practice for people with injuries or the elderly because it has slow and methodical movements, which help balance the brain and calm the nerves.

Mindfulness-Based Stress Reduction

"Mindfulness-based stress reduction" has been bubbling up in the news a fair amount for a couple of reasons. The first is because there have been some good studies showing how well it works for stressed-out patients.[8] That's a great thing. The second isn't as cool. It's been a way for psychiatrists trying to make a name for themselves to rebrand meditation and make it the latest "look at me, I'm so cool" technique.

It's essentially meditation with a scientific name so doctors can recommend it without getting browbeaten by their peers. That said, meditation works, so let's move on to the thing that's the centerpiece of the practice.

Meditation

Ah, meditation.

It's such an exquisite concept that people try to grasp yet often don't bother to explore. We commonly see emojis of people in lotus posture or Buddha statues in front of houses, but is that meditation?

Of course not.

Never confuse the map with the terrain.

Meditation is a way of being. It's an operating system. At the root of our being, there's stillness and peace. It's the essence of who we are.

Yet it's so elusive.

We all seem to grasp that *conceptually* meditation is something that we'd like to enjoy, but we don't always want to do the work. That's the problem. Most people want the outcome but are unwilling to actually sit there and *practice* meditation.

Yes, it's work.

It is a practice. That means you need to do it daily.

"I don't have time to practice something that will bring me peace, calm my nervous system, help me sleep better, relax my internal organs, help me make better decisions, and essentially fix my life. I'm too busy running around wondering why my life doesn't work!"

Have you met this person?

Hungry ghosts. Everywhere.

The practice of meditation involves doing something.

Doing what?

Essentially nothing. Just sit there and breathe and observe. Okay, now what?

Keep doing that until you start to come back to sanity.

People who have a regular practice can attest to the life-changing magic of meditation. Things begin to work out. Your health starts to shift for the better. You make good decisions. You are calm, collected, and capable of steering your life instead of tumbling around in the white water.

Meditation is the practice of *stopping time*. We essentially sit in a quiet place and do lower abdominal breathing. This, in turn, helps trigger our PNS, which keeps us in the "rest and digest" side of our nervous system.

It allows our body to relax and heal.

It helps drive blood and energy to the prefrontal cortex, which helps us with decision-making and the negation of impulses.[9]

It calms the mind and quiets all the reactions we have to the myriad dramas that are flung our way each day.

Once you understand that meditation is the root practice and operating system of choice, then any other practices you have become a moving form of meditation. We anchor in stillness and learn to move with it. It becomes the eye of the storm, the central pivot of our lives. Then our mind-body movement is a thing of beauty. From there we ripple out further into our exercise, our sleep, our family life, and every other corner of our Life Garden.

Meditation gives us the laserlike focus we need to direct our Water to the important areas of our lives. It helps us stay sane when the world is spinning, and it helps us say no when trouble comes knocking.

TIME COMPRESSION SYNDROME

When the walls are caving in and we have more commitments than time to fulfill them, that's what I call "Time Compression Syndrome," and it's an epidemic.

Perhaps you're worried about the future and living in the past. Your commitments slide you out of the present, and your time is always running thin. You're wound up and bound to a day that will never end and a list that keeps growing. You're being pulled into a future that keeps your feet moving even as you apologize for being late and disappointing people.

None of us wants to be a liar.

Nobody wants to be a flake.

We want to maintain our honor.

We want to maintain our integrity.

We know that's the right way to be and the type of person our parents raised us to be.

But we are lost.

It's time to take it all back.

Living in compressed time sucks. The way out is to *stop committing to new things*. Trim your yeses with strong, intentional nos that hold the line for what you really need to do that day and for what you choose to get out of life.

I'm going to help you get all the right tools in your belt, but I cannot do the work for you.

You need to meditate.

There's no way around doing the work. It's the pathway to an intentional life. Once you've been doing it for a while, you'll feel it working.

Just meditate.

GRATITUDE PRACTICE

Meditation puts you in the silent, eternal space that's your birthright. Gratitude broadcasts a signal of goodness and abundance to the heart of the Universe. Together, they are the most powerful combo humanity has known and the essential operating system of a person who's living an intentional life.

Gratitude signals abundance, the opposite of lack.

Many of us are stuck in a pattern of thinking our life, our circumstances, and our lot in life isn't good enough.

We *want*.

Whether what we want is material stuff, power, status, hair, a mate, or a pet monkey, *want* is an ugly energy. It's a slap in God's face that declares that what we currently have is not enough and that we're not grateful for it.

That's a fundamental mistake, and it'll keep draining you your whole life.

If you build your Life Garden as a wish list for all the things you're annoyed you haven't gotten yet, it won't work.

Let me repeat: it will not work.

Getting the life you want must begin with finding peace and gratitude for the life you currently have, even if you feel things suck.

Say your spouse left you and you have chronic pain and migraines. But there's food on the table, you've got a couple of good kids, and your cat is awesome. Giving thanks for these things each day sends a signal to the far reaches of the Universe that you're on point; you're in the game. That's a start.

All this stuff that matters to us is simply a holographic projection of thoughts that have assembled into matter.

There's more space between each atom than there is material stuff.

The river of Life is flowing through us. It's infinite in power and grace.

We understand so precious little about the reality we live in that it's embarrassing. Once you develop a meditation practice, you'll begin to get a glimpse. You'll start to understand how your thoughts create your reality and how *habitual thoughts* are a force of nature. All this will be proven to you in the workshop of life once you start playing the game right. That means dropping the BS, taking very good care of yourself and your health, and, yes, showing gratitude for everything you have in your life.

What we don't realize when we come from our egos is that we're not the ones driving. When I got out of the way and asked, "What does God want done?" life got grand. No project was too big after I realized I wasn't doing it for me. You too must get out of the way and let God, your Higher Self, the Universe, or whatever you want to call it drive your actions.

God—whatever that may be to you—is a broken and misused word that's caused much harm. But if you choose to close your eyes and dig into the silence, filling your heart with gratitude and warmth, there's a connection to something that emerges, something that's always been there, that's very familiar. Ride that feeling and explore it. Once you feel the presence, you will simply *know*.

The practice is quite simple. Grab a notebook, and spend just a few minutes thinking about the things you're grateful for each morning upon rising and each night before going to bed. Write them down, but not just in some "get my homework done quickly" way. Spend a few seconds or minutes on each item, and feel the gratitude in your heart.

At first, it may feel silly. That's fine—at first meditation is hard too. Just stay with it and let the gratitude warm your heart. It'll take hold over time and change you in ways you can't fathom right now. Just do it.

TITHING AND GIVING

Another aspect of the gratitude practice is giving back. Just like how thankfulness opens you up to the Universal flow, giving to charity and those in need does the same. First off, it's the right thing to do. People are desperate and need help. We are our brother's keeper. We need to look after one another.

This plugs us into the cycle of symbiosis, the interrelated web of interactions among species that work to mutually benefit each other. It's everywhere in nature, and we're a part of that web. From the bacteria in our guts that help us digest and fight off infections to the primal symbiotic relationship we have with mitochondria, which help us produce energy, we're all about teamwork.

Don't wall up. Don't isolate. This is the cycle. This is the *flow* of life.

Giving gives you energy.

Don't do it with the expectation of getting anything back; that's gross. Just do it and trust that it's the right thing to do. When you're giving from the heart, you're in the flow. When you're in the flow, good things come your way.

Share them, and keep it flowing.

You may want to consider adding some form of giving to your Life Garden plan as you construct it.

PLUGGING BACK INTO THE GARDEN

As we learn to calm our minds, we start to live in the PNS "rest and digest" Energy Economy. This helps us make better decisions in lifestyle and mental hygiene. As each department in your Vitality company flickers to life and becomes stable, more energy and Water become available for our Life Garden.

For now, this energy and Water go to the plants that you've already selected. Since things up until now may have been clunky, our first priority is to get things running smoothly.

Let's get some solid wins for you.

As your energy begins to increase, bring up the flow equally to all the areas of your Garden. Spend more time with your family, lift weights, take that extra hike, read a couple of books, paint that thing you've been meaning to get to—whatever is there in front of you. Pour your new energy into the areas of your life that need it, and stay on target.

Once things are full, robust, thriving, and happy, that's the time to consider either adding new items to your Garden or extending existing ones.

Do you have the patience and the self-worth to strive for stupendous results?

You should. And if you don't yet, you will.

You need energy.

You need focus.

Right now, you are laying the foundation for what you need to make your Life Garden grow.

QUANTUM ENERGY IS JUST UNDER THE SURFACE

A traditional power plant takes something, burns it, and uses the heat to drive turbines that generate electricity. It's clunky, dirty, and extraction-oriented.

Now what about hydroelectric? This has been a powerful innovation in science that takes an existing source of energy and uses it to generate electricity. The old windmills and watermills of antiquity reflect an early understanding of this. It isn't new.

Wind can turn a turbine and generate power.

Water flowing down a stream is a force of nature and can do the same.

We've taken this to a grand scale in modern times. We've built enormous dams and tapped nature's might to generate power we can send down lines to our houses. This has come at a cost, of course, as we've filled valleys and shifted habitats along the way, but most would argue that it's the cleanest source of power we've got until we can crack the code on a globally scalable solution—solar, wind, geothermal, fusion, or whatever tech solution emerges.

Now let's think about this in terms of our own bodies.

The entire Universe has a flow. There are gamma waves, X-rays, heat, sound, light, and whatever other particles and waves are moving and fluxing around us at all times. They penetrate our cells, the intracellular space, and the vast space between our atoms.

There's a powerful current of energy moving through us right now.

How can we tap into it and "generate" energy for ourselves?

How can we find the mini dams in our bodies where this flow is stuck and unblock it?

When you develop a meditation practice, you begin to feel the flow of this "force" that pervades the Universe all around you. In doing so, you begin to understand the fluid nature of your existence and the wondrous joke of how silly it is to take yourself so seriously.

There is power everywhere.

It is here and now.

If you learn to silence your mind and feel it, you are in the game.

You can learn to tap into the eternal power that flows through you and energize yourself—your mind, body, spirit, dreams, and future.

Lack is just a perception.

Tap into the eternal moment, and find the currents that are flowing through you. You can learn to generate energy from this, much like a watermill sitting on top of a stream.

MORE ENERGY = MORE TIME (ROUND TWO)

We've come full circle. You now understand why energy is needed in your life, and you at least understand why meditation is a good idea. Now let's talk about it in the context of time.

When you're time compressed, you are out of the flow. The energy of panic, scarcity, fear, drama, and overall lack is the central theme of the "fight or flight" operating system. That's not abundance.

What is abundant is the "rest and digest" vibe that helps us live in a timeless space. This is where higher-level thinking, creativity, and spontaneous laughter come from. We're at ease and not bound to time.

As you make your lifestyle more efficient, fix your sleep, reduce your stress, and exercise more, you'll start feeling better.

Work will be done sooner.

Errands will become more efficient, or you'll have more money to pay for help.

You'll wake up charged and ready to go.

You'll be better at the things you do, and you'll crush it in life.

Which all means that *you'll have more time on your hands.*

Warning: don't blow it.

In our culture of running around trying to look busy, it's really easy to get caught up. When you get a spare moment, it's easy to plug into your phone and find distractions instead of closing your eyes and breathing or simply watching people and enjoying the downtime.

Downtime is the enemy of our current world.

Take that downtime.

Savor it.

Make it a part of your day.

Sure, you can invest some of your newfound time into your Life Garden areas; that's the point. That said, you'll find time here and there that you will want to squander. That's simply a bad habit you need to become aware of so you can avoid it.

Daydreaming and Personal Growth

Getting to know who you truly are takes time. It takes *downtime*. It takes daydreaming, sketching, naps, hikes, silent drives, and plenty of meditation. As you get more time in your life, make sure you allow for some of this slow, "unproductive" stuff to get oxygen. This is where the real magic happens.

Don't be ashamed to relax and daydream.

Take the time and enjoy the moment.

PROPULSION

For all of the work it took to develop the rockets and technology to get us to the moon, millions of people lay on their backs and dreamt of it first. Eventually our curiosity led us to learn about the planet, gravity, and physics. But for thousands of years, we pondered our existence, the stars, and the grand scheme of things. Our quest began with a sense of awe and wonder. That was the impetus. It was the seed that got watered.

We can do anything we apply ourselves to. But we need a plan, a dream, or a destination.

Without meaning and purpose, we're lost in the world. We aimlessly look to material things to fill the void. We latch on to other people's plans and dreams because we are ashamed to admit that we lack our own. We fill our tanks and give the fuel to others who have better clarity. Worse, we fill our tanks and let them explode into chaos—again and again.

Enough of that.

Let's help you find focus and purpose.

LIFE GARDENING HOMEWORK

Before you begin your homework, I'd like you to visit a page I've created with links to free resources that will help you anchor in a mind-body practice. All of these are based on practices with an unbroken chain of transmission that spans thousands of years down the various lineages I've studied with. They are time-tested and pure. The meditations are simple, and the Qigong will take less than a few days to learn after following my lead. I invite you to download them and use them daily. The sooner you memorize them, the sooner you'll be free of needing a device in order to relax. You won't need me, an app, or any references to have a practice you call your own. You will be free.

Start using these resources immediately, and we'll work together to devise a plan to include them in your life so you can reap the rewards daily.

Please go to theurbanmonk.com/focus for the free downloads on meditation and Qigong.

GRATITUDE PRACTICE

The practice of gratitude is quite simple as long as you're not hurrying through it or faking it.

Grab a notebook, and spend just a few minutes thinking about the things you're grateful for each morning upon rising and each night before going to bed.

Write them down, but not in a "get my homework done quickly" way. Just keep writing and jotting down all the things you feel grateful for.

Spend a few seconds or minutes on each item, and feel the gratitude in your heart. Really feel it. It won't work unless you do this step. You have to really, truly feel grateful for the things in your life to change your state of being.

Just stay with it, and let the gratitude warm your heart.

Put a smile on your face and then move on. It'll take hold over time and change you in ways you can't fathom right now.

GIVING PRACTICE

Think of the ways you'd feel best giving back. It could be through a soup kitchen, your church, a school, community service, beach cleanup, or a youth program. We all need to be doing more to help solve the world's and our community's problems. Time, money, and energy are all valuable assets in this exchange, so if you're short on one, try one of the other forms of giving.

A few bucks here and there can transform a life, and giving some of your time can really help somebody. Do a search for groups or organizations, whether in your area or elsewhere, that speak to you or where your passion lies, and see how you can get involved. You'll meet other people doing good deeds, and your worldview will profoundly change. Do it now and don't procrastinate.

CHAPTER SEVEN

FINDING MEANING AND PURPOSE

We live in a declarative culture. At the ripe age of 18, we're asked to pick a path for our future and declare what we want to be for the rest of our lives.

It's *what*, not who.

What we do is a *what*. The role we play in society is a *what*.

Who we are is a precious luxury few have time to ponder.

Who we are is a great mystery—one worth exploring and contemplating.

Most people are so caught up in the minidramas of their life's circumstances that they never get a chance to get into the real work: *self-discovery*.

The part of us that's trapped in time is the part that can't bother to fathom such nonsense. Instead it'll pass the time decompressing in front of a TV, falling further asleep by the day. This eventually rusts our minds and robs us of any motivation to grow, so we sink until we're six feet under.

Meaning and purpose are elusive and hard to grasp.

They are funny words that we've been taught are important and things we ought to seek in order to have a fulfilling life.

Maybe.

Or maybe not.

Seeking meaning sucks. It feels contrived and forced.

Some people just feel it; they know what their purpose is and are living life accordingly.

Lucky bastards.

Some people may have a clue, but they are stumbling through life doing their best and perhaps waiting for an omen—some lightning bolt from above.

Others have given up completely. Nihilism, materialism, cultural pessimism, racism, religious bigotry, and several other "positions" are born of this. People either give up on meaning or, instead of searching for it, take a story they're given and run with it, if they don't kill for it.

But that's primitive and unbecoming of who we truly are. We need to question reality and explore it with wonder.

That is the way.

THE RAT RACE

Are you going to be a "doctor person" when you grow up? How about a "banker person" or "music person"? Perhaps you'll be a tradesperson—plumbing, electrical, and carpentry are all noble professions.

Whatever you choose, it typically means you'll hang with similar people and identify with their likes, from their favorite teams to their politics. Dinner parties become a chorus, and even music choices start to blend. These are your people, unlike those *other people*.

It's all so trite, yet it's the reality we are stuck in.

It's fine on the periphery until people start taking it way, way, way too seriously. Enter the lynchings, the suicide bombs, the angry rallies—the basic "we're better than them" thing that's so pervasive in our culture taken to a sick level. Intolerance is a sign of the breakdown of symbiosis and civility. It'll be our end.

We're better than *that*—individually and collectively.

So let's set an example and be a guiding light by finding it for ourselves first.

START WITH THE BASICS

There's no way you can feel well, let alone think clearly about your future, when you lack energy. Have you ever had depressing thoughts when you caught the flu? Of course you have. When there's no energy, life's problems seem bigger and more in your face.

It's the same with life's big questions. You can't really have a positive lock on your meaning and purpose in life if you don't feel so hot. In fact, when you have a lack of Vitality, pessimism and fear take over your operating system.

We are a reflection of our bodies.

If you're lacking in Vitality and trying to pound through the challenging task of figuring out your meaning in life, I'd like to ask you to *stop right now*. We cannot explore our self-awareness and consciousness if we're focused on survival.

If you are afraid for your life living in the neighborhood you're in or worried about ethnic cleansing after reading the news, it's tugging at your survival instinct. That stress is driving your consciousness away from higher-order systems in the brain and toward panic mode.

Real stress—whether emotional, physical, financial, or psychological—hits us biologically and pushes us into the amygdala and back to fight or flight.

Many people have bought their way out of the "time for money" exchange but are caught up in another rat race—bigger cars, fancy parties, showing off—and still stuck without meaning.

Getting healthy and fit doesn't solve all of life's problems. Neither does getting out of debt and being financially stable. But these things can help you get to a place where you can plug your energy into doing the real work.

Once you attain a baseline level of Vitality, the real work can start, and that work is deeply personal. It requires downtime, silence, time in nature, journaling, and contemplation. It may require making amends with people in your past and taking the leap on trying new things. It may require cutting your spending and getting your money game together. There are many ways to climb the mountain, but one thing is for sure: you'll need some baseline energy and a good night's sleep before attempting it. Start there.

STOP TRYING TO FIT IN

The next stop on this journey is to cut the crap.

Whether it's a religion, a philosophy, a political ideal, a fan club, or whatever else, people are looking for somewhere to belong and feel less alone. Buying blindly into any of these scripts will inhibit your ability to think clearly and freely about your own destiny.

Everyone is looking for followers, and these systems operate as a catch basin to grab the masses. Let me be clear: not all are bad. Feeding people at soup kitchens, doing mission work, cleaning up beaches, and keeping our kids off the street are all noble things and should be encouraged. That said, when these activities are tied to a cultural or religious identity, it can limit our free thinking, individuality, and ability to find our actual meaning and purpose. All I ask is that you become aware of this possibility and catch any places where fitting in is actually stifling your personal growth and freedom.

IT'S OKAY TO BE STRANGE

With all the headlines about climate change, social unrest, new viruses, the rise of fascism, and the constant threat of nuclear war, it's hard to remain calm about the state of the world. Many things are obviously not so great, and we don't seem to be headed in a positive direction on the planet.

On the other hand, there's the promise of new technologies that can help us out and the spirits of millions of people galvanizing around what's right for our children. It is a time of extreme polarity, unrest, and, yes, *hope.*

Hope.

Everything in nature fights to survive; that's the programming. This applies to bacteria all the way up to human-made industries that are polluting the planet. The latter take on lives of their own as they generate money, jobs, lobbyists, and influence. They too fight to survive even if their existence no longer serves humanity or the planet. They do everything they can to stop the inevitable.

Now is not the time to fit right in.

It's not the time to blindly look away and hope "they" fix the world's problems. There is no "they"—it's you. You are at the center of all your problems, and the mere fact that you're witnessing these things makes you accountable to do something about it.

Complacency is not an option.

As we get into this broader conversation about meaning and purpose, I want to make something very clear. It doesn't mean running for the hills and hiding out where the world's problems can't find you. There's nowhere to run or hide. This is our fight and our opportunity to step up and make things right.

As we tap into what we're passionate about, it may bring us headlong into a fight over water, air, frogs, gender rights, or whatever else you are interested in or infuriated by.

People think that finding meaning means dropping out and wandering the earth. It means ignoring the world's struggles. That's a misread of scripture.

Jesus Christ was a renegade rabbi who vehemently rebelled against the corruption of his day. He was outspoken, bold, and aggressive, galvanizing a core group around him, which eventually led to the formation of the world's largest religion, one that preaches love and tolerance.

The Shaolin Buddhist monks learned kung fu and became the warrior monks of China. They defended the innocent and oftentimes upheld their values with the use of the sword to fight evil tyrants and protect the weak.

There are hundreds of examples of this in history, where people didn't sit around. They stood for their beliefs and were passionate about them. That's part of this "meaning and purpose" conversation as well.

We must confront evil and fight for what's good and right in this world.

We're often made to believe spirituality is about sitting on a rock, starving ourselves, and letting go of the world. That's the perfect storyline for someone who wants to maintain control.

But as you dig into the emotions and feelings that bring you joy and make you feel alive, you may face the challenge of feeling strange from going against the grain. If you want to make a change about something you're passionate about, you may risk alienating some people and standing out. Your purpose may require that of you, so be prepared.

It's okay. We need the weird you much more than the half-alive version of you that's afraid of truly living life and speaking up.

Step up. Now is the time to be a hero.

EXPERIENCES VS. THINGS

I've met a lot of people who mistake the meaning of life with the things they pick up along the way. The "good life" means having the house, the vacations, and cars, the *stuff* that makes life easier and more enjoyable. Sure, that stuff can help. Jets are great when trying to cross the country; that's a long drive.

Dishwashers are awesome; they give you your time back. The question becomes, *"Time to do what?"*

Are you getting time back to meditate or make love to your spouse? Cool.

Or is it time to binge-watch some drama on Netflix and diminish your sleep quality?

Does your smartphone help you manage your calendar, avoid traffic, and listen to audiobooks and learn more? Great.

Or are you playing *Candy Crush* to avoid your day?

Worse yet, are you scrolling Instagram and looking at the fake versions of real people's lives—the story they want you to believe about them?

These tools we've invented are not inherently bad. They help us make life better when used for the right reasons and can absolutely be tools to help us have a better life.

The issue arises when we practice *idolatry*. That's when we elevate these things to a level where we think they intrinsically bring us happiness, where we mistake the map for the terrain.

Despite efforts by Egyptian pharaohs to take their loot to the afterlife, I'm pretty sure that it didn't work. They left the planet, and grave robbers got the gold, cups, and cat statues.

You can't take the stuff with you.

The experiences, however, those are ours for life—and possibly beyond. They make up the stories that bring color to our lives. They make us interesting and help us engage with other people. They are the adventures we can write and read about, the tales that we can relate to and laugh about.

They are the currency of life's richness and add joy and beauty to our lives. That said, many of us are stuck watching actors playing them out on TV.

Life is to be lived and is not a spectator sport.

If you want greater meaning in your life, you're going to have to live it.

That means planning that trip.

It means taking the dance or karate class.

It means taking the bold step of going somewhere you've always dreamt of going.

These are all under the Life's Passions section of your Life Garden. These are the unresolved desires that have yet to be expressed fully. We have lots of regrets around this area, and many of us have simply given up. Life's troubles, bills, the kids, or whatever else has gotten in the way, and now we can't afford to be a "dreamer."

That's nonsense.

It's time to tiptoe back into each of these items and figure out how to drip some Water onto them.

People often think that there's some sort of "hammer in the head" action that can deliver meaning and purpose down from a column of white light from Heaven. Pow! Okay, now you have a mission and know who you are—go forth and be!

That's bullshit. Moses was in deep prayer and climbed the mountain to have his encounter. Christ traveled through the Middle East and India performing austerities and doing the work along the way. Mohammad fasted and prayed in a mountain cave. It was work.

Again, don't be afraid to do the work. What's been elusive to you may be so because it isn't designed to come to you . . . you have to walk to it.

Follow your inspiration.

Meaning and purpose can be found in the little things that inspired you as a kid. They are locked away under the distractions you've amassed on top of your busy schedule.

We've all got things that are of interest to us, things that make us passionate. Whether it's art, music, space, oceans, psychology, or weaving, it's somewhere in you, and there lies your first clue toward meaning and purpose.

One thing is for sure: it's not in the actual things.

For example, let's say you've always wanted a horse and a ranch. These are both *things* for sure. Now, is it that you intrinsically want these things in and of themselves, or is there a feeling and lifestyle associated with owning them?

You love how you feel on a horse. It's such a noble animal; you feel connection and affinity, a real bond. The fresh air in your face when you're riding it, the trees all around, the rivers and streams out in the wild—yes, yes, yes, the horse and you are so happy out there.

Where?

The ranch, of course. It's far, far away from the city, and it's quiet and away from all the noise and stress.

Okay, so do you really want a horse and ranch, or are you craving the *experience* of peace in a natural setting where you can relax and find serenity?

Are you longing for connection with another lifeform who will not disappoint you?

As we map out the things we think we need to be happy—the things we think are going to bring us peace, meaning, and purpose—let's make sure we dig into the underlying feelings and experiences we actually crave behind the things we say we want. Without this level of clarity, we're lost in a world of endless consumption that will leave us wanting in perpetuity.

COLLECTING THINGS VS. SMILE WRINKLES

Have you ever met someone with beautiful wrinkles on their face? You know, the ones that have come from years of smiling with their mouths, cheeks, eyes, and brows? You can instantly see their personality, happiness, peace, and kindness in their face. It's been etched into their complexion from a lifetime of happiness and good living.

This, to me, is a beautiful thing. It's a mark of a life filled with stories, kindness, and experiences that makes this person radiate. Now contrast that with a person who spent their life buying things they don't need and sent more and more garbage into the landfills that are vomiting up yesteryear's junk already.

It's a bad deal—foolish actually.

The mass-consumption ideology that's pervasive in our culture has been fed to us by the companies that make and manufacture all that *stuff.* They need buyers. The system needs your time and energy in the form of money in order to stay alive. It's a pipe dream, and it's driving our extinction.

Instead, work on finding the experiences that make you happy, and go live your life fully.

There's a difference between needs and wants, and the advertising industry's job is to make us believe all those myriad *wants* are actually *needs*. Wake up and smell the mouse trap.

Let's focus on creating those smile wrinkles and getting time with our loved ones. Let's focus on a life filled with trips, adventures, cuddling with kids and dogs, and reading good books.

Let's focus on what matters.

MUSIC IS THE SILENCE BETWEEN THE NOTES

If you fill your life with things and noise, you can never hear the beauty of Creation in the stillness. If you live in the amygdala and are constantly stressing over the daily grind, you can't relax into the eternal peace of the living Universe.

We have to leave room for magic in our lives, and that happens with stillness, with time to relax and molt. You may be thinking, "Yeah, yeah, that sounds cute, but let's get back to the practical. Stop wasting my time."

That's your time-compressed stress brain talking.

We're so accustomed to being stressed and wound up, we only want to hear what we think we need to hear as we scavenge reality desperately searching for "food" in our survival state.

Pure art never came from this level of consciousness. Neither did great lovemaking or amazing literature.

Peace is elusive when we come from our amygdala and hindbrain. So is enlightenment, and that's the problem.

We've been blessed and cursed with a prefrontal cortex. Our brains have developed to a level where we've become self-aware and conscious of our own existence. That's the double-edged sword that leads to both enlightenment and depression. It's the path to peace and abundance or dark, confusing thoughts.

THE PATH TO PURPOSE

If you want to talk about purpose, you'll need energy and Vitality to come off life's breadline, and then you'll need to activate the prefrontal cortex.

Higher-order functions like morality, self-awareness, conscious planning, and certainly the contemplation of our existence all come from parts of our brain that are unique to humans. It's possible that dolphins have some of this too, and there's some interesting research looking at this, but for our purposes, you're it.

It can be argued that humans are the highest form of expression of evolution on this planet. But then why are we so stupid?

Wars, pollution, corruption, racism, and bigotry—how are these expressions of our evolution?

They are not.

Then how can we come out of our amygdala dominance and rise up to our prefrontal cortex?

Never—unless we take on an active practice of reversing this trend.

A mind-body practice is like mental floss. Without it, there's rot and decay everywhere. There's a worldview that's gloomy, pessimistic, and fear inspired. We're constantly driven toward the lowest common denominator of a struggle for resources, "might makes right," and "get yours over theirs" survival. It's so pervasive that we become fish, not knowing what water is because we live and breathe it.

Unless we do something about it.

ENHANCE AND EXPAND YOUR CONSCIOUSNESS

You can't derive what your meaning or purpose should be if you're in a trance about what life's about.

We need to elevate and find our inner compass—our core morality and our deepest sense of peace and happiness that comes from knowing who we are.

Don't let anybody tell you who you are. That's for you to discover. It's the magical journey that'll unlock joy, happiness, mysteries, and, yes, possibly your purpose in life. It comes from tapping into the silence and stilling your mind.

Once we learn how to separate from the noise and *not react*, we can *observe* the noise and remain still. Within that stillness, there's a certain something. It will be very faint at first, but we can sense it. We sit with that. We continue to breathe and cultivate stillness. Then we begin to hear it or see it—the inklings, the feelings.

Just sit.

Tap into the eternal stillness of the present moment, and *observe*.

Just observe.

You'll know it when you are there.

Time stops.

You feel at home.

There's a feeling of familiarity and comfort.

And then it will be gone.

You might grasp and struggle to get it back.

Don't.

Go back to stilling your mind and watching your breath. Your next visit may have a completely different quality to it. You may feel joy. Or it may bring up past trauma or old regrets. Perhaps a memory from your childhood or a flash of inspiration.

Do not grasp.

Stay in the stillness, and bask in the sunlight of your third eye.

Afterward, go ahead and journal and take notes.

The key is to continue to tap into this state and direct more and more neurons in its direction. This is the "Stairway to Heaven," the "Golden Flower," and the "Eternal Gate" that the ancients spoke of. It's a real thing. The only way you'll know is to do the practice. Reading about it alone will *never* get you there.

You must do the work and cultivate stillness. I call this cultivating the "vertical axis," which is the chakra, or *dantian*, system of the Far East. We still our minds and become aware of our inner anatomy of energy centers, which then opens the portal to all of life's great power and mystery. Then you'll see that the world's drama and noise are dark distractions from the inner radiance, peace, and beauty that are your birthright.

You must still your mind and stop time.

This is when you'll know you are reversing the "fight or flight" drive of our world and pulling blood and energy up from your hindbrain to your higher brain centers and prefrontal cortex.

This is just the start—the homecoming to your evolutionary birthright. Anything before this will have been contaminated by survival struggles, reactivity, mind chatter, and infectious cultural memes that tell us what to do or who to be. These things go unquestioned and sneak right under our radar.

You have to turn on the light of your awareness and examine your own mind. Once you settle through the noise and maddening chaos, ride that wave and never stop.

With more clarity, you'll have more focus.

With more focus, you'll be better at curating the plants in your Life Garden.

With better curation and focus, you'll stay on point with feeding Water to each area and seeing your plants grow and thrive.

With this comes more energy, abundance, peace, family and friend connections, and Vitality.

With this added Vitality, you'll maintain your focus and continue to *curate* your Garden and make your life actually work.

When life is good, you move beyond survival. This happens on a monetary, energetic, social, societal, and deep, inner level.

As you release the trauma and truly come to a place of peace and stillness, you then have the clarity and foresight to navigate life better.

You have more time.

You invest that time in enjoying the stillness and exploring who you truly are.

Then the "Spiritual Gold" is upon you. Bask in its sunshine.

ASCETICS VS. HOUSEHOLDERS

In the ancient religions of Asia, there were two main tracks for people to follow: the path of the ascetic and that of the householder. I wrote about this in my book *The Urban Monk*. We need to address it here, as I feel it's a fundamental misreading of scripture and leads to unnecessary suffering.

Ascetics go off to the monasteries. They renounce material possessions, often take vows of celibacy, and give their lives to "the Work." They perform austerities all day and essentially have the full-time job of "figuring life out." They get to sit around and cultivate stillness all the time and are tasked with "holding it down" for society. A very small percentage of the population has historically taken this path over the years—far less today than before.

So what about everybody else?

They are householders. Historically, that meant they picked a craft, got a job, made money, dealt with bills, made and raised babies, and somehow, when they had some time, cultivated stillness and found inner peace. In India, householders worked all their lives and in their "golden years" would go up to the monasteries and cultivate their spiritual lives after having fulfilled their obligations to their families and to the world. In our current world, we work our asses off and then get shipped to retirement communities, where we work on our golf swing and gossip with others. I call this the "horizontal axis," where we live in the world, feed off each other, and forget we have a spiritual nature until we have the luxury of thinking about it later in life . . . and yet we don't.

In our current culture, we're pretty much all sitting here as householders feeling guilty for not making a 90-minute yoga class and being able to meditate all the time. We have lofty dreams, but that money thing keeps coming up. We want to go explore, but we've got those kids. Darn. The cool, flashy stories of spirituality and enlightenment came to us from the East, yet we took them out of context.

Nobody with a career has all day to sit around and meditate, so how do householders find balance, peace, meaning, and purpose with all of their other obligations in place?

The core deal: we have to get our shit together and then find our true self now.

We have to become masters at life so we have the energy, time, patience, and clarity to "find ourselves" in all the noise right here and now while life is happening all around us.

This is why, over the years, I've found the Life Garden work to be so meaningful and successful. We're not here to run away from our lives. We've got houses, cars, power bills, and student loans. These cost money. Money takes time or effort to make.

Kids? Lord knows they cost money and take all kinds of time.

We're tangled in the web of life, and we're looking for a way out of the mess we're in.

But the way out is *in*.

Let's flip the script. As you get into the essential mapping and planning of your Life Garden in the next chapter, keep in mind that you're dealing with plants you've allowed in there. If you identify something as a weed, stop watering it. In Chapter 8, we'll work on ways to untangle the weeds and get clear about what must remain.

But what about the plants we decide get to stay?

It's time to craft an elegant solution that, slowly but surely, starts to turn things around. If I plant things in my physical, backyard garden, depending on the species, I usually see the harvest in about 90 days. That's in real life, but it also works the same for your Life Garden. Habits take time to change. Things need time and energy to grow. We have to *consistently* water them, and that requires focus.

That's why each Gong we do is 100 days. We need to be patient and let nature take its course. We can't just get out of the way, though.

A good gardener checks the soil daily. They look at the plants and make sure each is getting water. They weed out invaders and bless the garden and send loving energy to each plant they walk by. Nature and the miracle of life work to take the water and grow life in the garden, but we're here to help things along and curate what gets to thrive.

It is our Garden.

We get to choose.

As we make these choices, life gets better, and we're more on top of things. The householders go from struggling on life's breadline of time, money, and energy to being free to explore and manifest their dreams.

Once your plants get enough water and are cleared of weeds and noise, they take on a life of their own and root down further. Now they thrive on their own and need less attention. They become robust and grow strong thanks to your direction and early curation. The soil under your feet gets healthier and can hold more water and sustain more healthy bacteria. You keep an eye on it all, for sure, but it's more like smiling and greeting your plants tenderly as you casually stroll through the garden.

The toil has paid off.

This is the work. Get your life together, and then enjoy the harvest. Invest the time, money, and energy into further and further exploration of your inner stillness. From here, meaning and purpose emerge as a line of inquiry. It's from a place of peace—the "rest and digest" space of a happy human who has worked their way out of survival mode and daily strife.

Will shit hit the fan ever again?

Of course it will. This is life. However, you'll have the neuronal circuitry built in from years of good habits and meditation to have a very long fuse. Seasoned meditators are more mentally and emotionally resilient. They can handle pressure better because they live in a peaceful place and have the capacity to think clearly through a crisis.

This will be you.

Does this mean there is meaning or not?

There is no one answer. That's the treasure of life that's yours to explore. Perhaps the journey is all we need. Or maybe there's no need for actual meaning at all. Many believe that, and I don't think they're wrong. Life itself is filled with energy, light, love, joy, and pure bliss when you tap into the stillness and feel it. It is rich, full, and abundant, and it is whole in and of itself.

It simply is.

Perhaps we humans are searching for meaning because we're disconnected from the Source. I often think this when I see a deer happily chomping on grass in front of me.

He's there.

When I'm deep in meditation, I feel that. I'm simply there . . . or *here*. It's all right here. It's full of energy, joy, wisdom, and it feels like *life*.

Life has an energy, a feeling, a profound consciousness, a fullness, and a deep, deep sense of innate connection *with all other life*. That feeling—that *knowing*—is right here.

When you tap into it, there are no silly questions about "What's my purpose in life?" Those things, to me, seem to come from our minds and egos trying to feel less alone and afraid in this scary world. They seem to come from our incessant need to define ourselves and *be someone* so we feel significant in this scary place.

When we're tapped into the energy of life and love, all that goes away. We know who we are, and that "who" is somehow tied into all the other "whos" out there, including the rocks, the birds, and the stars. There's only one "who," and that's All of Us, the "I Am" of the Bible, the great Tao, the Universal Mind. This is the superconscious mind. Once you tap into the Universal intelligence, there's a stream of love and wisdom you have access to that's simple and true. It's been there all along, but we've been too spun out to hear it.

Listen.

When you tap into a meditation practice, you feel all the anxiety and stress of who you think you need to be go away. You relax into the "suchness" of your being and stop trying to find meaning. You're plugged in and feel the life all around you.

Does this mean you sit around like a smiling blob?

Sometimes.

But when you get stagnant, you go for a walk. You run into people and have a chance to smile and engage with them. You go to work and carry that peace and stillness into everything you do, letting it ripple into your industry and bring light to the people around you. You treat your children with kindness and raise them in a conscious, happy way. You let someone merge into your lane. You write inspired poetry. Perhaps you run for Senate.

Are you catching my drift?

Tap into your stillness and stop time *first*. Then carry that space into your everyday life with you and see how the journey unfolds. Perhaps you find something that is clearly what people from the outside say is your "calling" or "purpose," or perhaps you happily light up your own path without identifying this and enjoy a life filled with peace and joy.

It doesn't matter.

Stop worrying about it.

Just get your Garden together and cultivate stillness. Everything else will melt around you, and your illuminated consciousness will light your path effortlessly.

You know where you need to go. It all begins with your Life Garden. Now the work begins.

Let's calm your mind, boost your Vitality, and bring order to your Garden. From there, you'll have more and more time to ask the bigger questions and find your path in life. In my experience, the path has always been in front of us, but we've gotten so distracted and lost that we started looking for it instead of looking down at our own feet and coming back to the present moment.

The path is not far.
You're standing on it.
You can relax.
Now, we need to get your householder's affairs in order.
Let's map out your Life Garden.

LIFE GARDENING HOMEWORK

As you assemble your Life Garden, you're moving from where you've been to where you'd like to arrive.

We're going to probe into some areas that will help you better identify your passions and desires. Be honest with yourself and spend some time really thinking this through, as it'll form the seeds of your Life Garden.

MY PASSIONS

All the areas under the "Life's Passions" section of your Life Garden are the unresolved desires in your life that have yet to be expressed fully. Jot down what your passions are. What's on your bucket list—the things you must see, do, or accomplish before you die? Even if it sounds unrealistic, write it all down. We can map out a 10-year plan for some of this, if need be.

Jot down what comes to mind for the following areas:

What are my hobbies?
What are my special interests?
What types of books do I want to read?
Where would I like to travel, see, and go?
What sports do I like?
What causes do I support?
What types of movies do I like?
What else am I passionate about?

MY DESIRES

Make a list of the *things* you really want. Think about the list you create. Are these things you really want, or have you been trained or convinced to think or say you want them?

Will these things really make you happy? If so, then keep them on the list. If not, remove them. For the items you keep, leave space to the right of each one.

What are the material things that I desire in my life?

The Feelings and Experiences I Long For

As we map out the things we think we need to be happy—the things we think are going to bring us peace, meaning, and purpose—let's make sure we dig into the underlying feelings and experiences we actually crave behind the things we say we want. Without this level of clarity, we're lost in a world of endless consumption that leaves us wanting in perpetuity.

Go back to the list of desired objects, and next to each, write out the feeling or experience each one would provide you.

MY LIFE'S REGRETS

What are your major regrets?

We have lots of regrets in life, and many of us have simply given up. Life's troubles, bills, the kids, or whatever else has gotten in the way, and we feel we can't afford to be a "dreamer." Whether they were large or small, list what your life's major regrets have been.

This is all about pulling your passions out of you, so we need to come at it from different directions. Here are some additional questions that I'd like you to spend time with:

What's it going to take to get my Garden together?

What areas of my Garden are keeping me in survival mode?

Where am I being blindsided?

Why can't I relax? Where is that coming from?

What do I need to feel safe?

How can I build a meditation practice into my life?

What else can point me to my true passion in life?

Once you've completed this section, put it away for a night, and come back to it the following day. Read over it and see what you can add. See what you can glean from what you've written, and spend a few more minutes thinking about each area. Sadly, we spend precious little time thinking about the key questions in life, although we live life daily. Let's take a long look at our passions, desires, and regrets before we make a plan that we commit to. It's hard to get behind a 100-day plan when things we never thought about keep bubbling up and confounding everything.

You need *all of you* on board in order to have a plan for your Life Garden that you will want to stick to. A hundred days is a long time, but if you shortchange an aspect of yourself, the work won't feel complete. When you get it all covered, you will be able to stick to your plan and make your Garden thrive.

CHAPTER EIGHT

ASSEMBLING YOUR 100-DAY GONG

Living life.

It's a bit more complicated than merely surviving. That is, *if you care*.

If you care about living an intentional, successful, healthy, full life, you have to stop stumbling around.

You need to pick yourself up and clean up your act. You've got to fix your sleep; you need to be mindful about what you eat; you need to build muscle mass and move your body; and you unequivocally need to develop a practice that flips the switch from SNS to PNS dominance.

You need your third eye—the prefrontal cortex—to be alive, alert, activated, and working to help you suppress impulsive decisions. You need to remember what you wanted for yourself yesterday when today's wave of distractions flood in.

Attention span is the key.

Vitality powers the system and drives your willpower.

Focused willpower taps the very power of Creation when we can sustain it.

Pick your plants, and remember to water them day in and day out.

Don't waver.

Look at the soil of your subconscious. Keep scanning for weeds—those nasty habits, beliefs, and negative memes that haunt us from our past.

Pull the weeds.

If they keep growing back, it means there's still a seed hidden, buried deep in your subconscious soil. It's okay. Keep weeding and pulling, and you'll eventually isolate the seed and pull it out. This is all yours to have if you keep going and keep doing the work.

Replace bad habits with good habits that serve you better.

Stay on your mind-body practices, and continue to live in "rest and digest." Train your body to relax. Train your mind to relax. Healing happens here. Good decisions come from here.

This covers a lot of ground—your ground. Your soil.

This is how you end up with a healthy Life Garden.

It's your life, your Garden.

Your time, money, and energy.

You are the only person who gets to direct it—and the only person who should. God gave us agency to decide for ourselves. We have the innate power of Creation embedded deep within us because we're a candle from the Original Flame. The more you awaken to this, the less separation you'll see and the more connected you'll feel to the Superconscious Mind, the Universe, the Mind of God—whatever you call it in your world.

Once you handle the householder basics and stop sweeping things under the rug, you'll come to realize that it's easier to *simply handle your shit.*

When the survival mode vice loosens, you'll think clearly, breathe deeply, rest fully, and enjoy your life. You'll stop making decisions out of duress, and you'll masterfully map out your life 100 days at a time. You'll look ahead and choose where you want to go, and with gas in the tank, you'll go there.

You'll still need the brakes of your prefrontal cortex to adjust your speed, avoid life's obstacles, and stay on the road.

If you do only some of this work and skip over the meditation, you're going to pump the brakes, and they're not going to be responsive.

Daily practice builds impulse control for you. Please don't forget this as your power increases and your life takes off.

FUTURE PACING YOUR LIFE

Now that you've spent time mapping out where you've been in each area of your Life Garden, it's time to look ahead. Navigation can only work when you've gotten your bearings and know where you currently stand. I trust you've done the work at the end of each chapter. If not, now is the time.

When we look ahead to your future, there are likely dozens of things you'd like to do, experience, acquire, or change. Some of these things may be big and take some time. There may be a five-year project with lots of moving parts. That's great. You simply need to manage expectations, check your Water levels, and make a plan to keep dripping Water there until it's done.

This entire framework is designed to help you set achievable goals and do 100-day sprints to get there. Each Gong, or 100-day sprint, will have its own 30-, 60-, and 100-day goals, with daily action items you set for yourself. What are the *specific actions* you can start taking today that will eventually get you there?

Then what are your goals and actions you will take in the next 30, 60, and 100 days to get you there?

How about in the next year?

If you find that you're kicking ass and surpassing expectations, then great. Keep building the areas you prioritized for that Gong, and see how much better you can do.

But first we're going to break down the big stuff into smaller chunks of actions. That's the secret: one bite at a time . . . but you have to start.

TAKING ACTION

Talk is cheap. Scan your social feeds. Everyone's got something to say, and everyone is moaning about this or that. How many people do you know who actually stand up and take action? How many people see a problem in front of them and get up and work to find a solution?

Life will throw things that can be construed as problems at us all day. A flat tire, a busted pipe, a fulfillment issue at work, a child in trouble at school, a medical diagnosis—these are all typically seen as problems or obstacles. They are bummers if we don't see them as opportunities to grow and learn and to become bigger, better, stronger, and more resilient in life.

Life is a workshop where we learn and grow. Again, the phrase *kung fu* translates as "hard work" or "eat bitter" in Chinese. This is all about life's toil and the work we do to solve problems.

Does it mean that life is supposed to be hard?

Kind of. Yes.

Life is hard.

A seed takes water in the soil and sprouts up with life, fighting to get to the surface and get some sunlight. From there it converts the rays of the sun into energy so it can continue to grow and get strong. Wind, rain, bugs, and scarcity are always issues for a young plant. It can get trampled or eaten by animals pretty early on. Once it grows, it continues to root and anchor, gaining strength and resilience. Does that mean there won't be another storm or issue?

Of course not.

Life keeps throwing challenges our way. That plant doesn't even have credit cards, traffic, or politics to deal with. But we humans often feel the need to fit in with our peers, worry about what to wear this weekend, and wonder why the icebergs are melting.

There is a fantasy out there that fools people into thinking that once they've "arrived," all their life's problems will go away. A big boat, hammock on a beach, shiny car, or fat bank account, and it will be nothing but smooth sailing. That's nonsense.

Easy come, easy go.

Lotto winners tend to lose their pot of gold. Rich people get cancer too. Kids die, and cars crash. Shit happens to everyone.

True wealth is *resilience* and *strength*.

It's about *resourcefulness* much more than resources.

When your kung fu is good, you don't fret over whether your opponent is going to throw a punch, kick, tackle, or even pull a gun. You're ready. You're ready for whatever comes because you're calm, well trained, collected, and awake.

This takes action.

In kung fu, it means continual training—staying fit, alert, and getting better at your art every day.

Do not be fooled into digging for fool's gold. There are droves of people searching for the missing manuscript or the perfect diet, exotic supplement, or guru—the one thing that'll change everything for them. That's nonsense.

Do the work.

There's a saying in Farsi: "From you, action; from God, grace."

Action.

That means if you have been talking about exercising, get up and do some now. If you're confused about your diet, your very next meal is an opportunity to turn it all around.

If you've been wanting to start a meditation practice and keep talking about it, *for God's sake*, just start. Close your eyes and do it now. Everything will still be here in 15 minutes when you open your eyes and come back.

Action.

Action means pulling your focus toward something and powering it with your intent. It gets the mitochondria cranking and the energy flowing in your body. Your brain solves for that specific problem, and your muscles move to make it happen. You are moving matter all around you, shifting the physical structure of the Universe as you exert your will to see something happen in the world.

This is important to understand. God handed us a paintbrush that we put down and forgot about. Action takes us out of our heads and *moves the Universe* around us. It takes our thoughts and dreams and sprouts them in reality, right there in front of us.

The more we prove to ourselves that we can do this, the less we're stuck in our heads and the clearer we become about who we truly are. There are a lot of cobwebs to work through, but eventually we see it.

We can create the life that we want.

Action turns magical when clarity is coupled with drive . . . when attention works with intention.

It's right there in front of you.

What's your vision?

Let's paint.

MAKE SURE IT'S THE LIFE YOU WANT

If you found a genie and were granted three wishes, what would they be and why?

It's an important exercise because we all know what happened to Aladdin. His wishes actually caused lots of drama.

Would your wishes create a stable, happy, peaceful, and fulfilling life?

You are the genie. You know this.

Clarity, focus, willpower, and action will get you there.

However, if you really want it, there's a price. Will your family suffer? How about your health or relationships?

One plant taking most of the Water starves out the rest of the Garden. You can certainly choose that. If your dream is big, realize that making that decision might mean saying good-bye to people and cutting ties. It's better to do it preemptively with good communication than to watch your life fall apart all around you in chaos. That can derail people too.

I'm certainly not recommending this approach, but if you use it, I can at least help you prepare for the fallout.

For most people, I've seen tremendous results with the "base hits," or getting your life together in each area and working to build more resilience, Vitality, and clarity. Over time, the soil gets healthier, and things begin to work out better. You will have more time, money, and energy to go around once you've figured out the householder thing.

Just make sure you look at the map before setting out on the road trip. You will get there faster with some planning.

RETROFLECTION

Retroflection is when you turn the light of awareness around and look inside. This is the essence of meditation and the roadmap to enlightenment. You must focus your gaze inward and learn about your essential nature, and you'll need to meditate to find the gold inside. This is the basis for the work we're doing with our Gongs.

Turn inward.

Examine your life, and pick what you want.

Make a plan to take daily action in that direction, and *stick with it.*

When we focus on something, our Shen is locked on it. Then the Qi, or energy, flows to that point in time and space, and the material world starts to assemble around it. Over time, the object of our focus manifests in reality. Now if you're really good, like Sai Baba, you can have that object magically appear in your hand.

Maybe.

I can't speak to that, as those stories are rare and far from most of our realities.

What I can speak to is your ability to assemble contractors, handymen, factories, manufacturing, publishing, or whatever's available to you right here on planet Earth to create what you see in your mind.

I'm going to hold your hand and help you get there, one step at a time, in 100-day sprints.

START WHERE YOU STAND

You are here now.

The next logical step is the first step to take.

As we get into mapping the action items and goals for your Gong, it's nice (and essential) to keep the ends in mind, but first we need to start with the *doable*, practical steps to get us there.

For example, if you have a bad hip, diabetes, and short-ness of breath, that's okay—it's where you are right now. It doesn't mean that you put "win a triathlon" in your 30-day goals. You can get there in a year, perhaps, but not 30 days. You've got work to do.

So then what would the 30-day goal look like?

Perhaps some hip stretches each morning followed by a 15-minute walk for exercise, a shift to whole foods with no sugar or alcohol for 30 days, no TV at night with a 9 P.M. sleep time, and a seated meditation practice for Mindset. That's more than enough. In 30 days, you'll be feeling a bit better, and you might be able to add push-ups and lunges.

Are you catching my drift?

You need a sustainable and doable plan that'll actually get you there versus pulling a muscle and busting your knee.

Let's say you really want to be rich but are buried in debt and have some issues with cash flow in your company.

I'd still say start with your health and Vitality and make sure that part of the Garden is thriving, and then take the nec-essary steps in the right sequence to get unstuck financially.

Can you cold call 10 people a day to drum up some flow? Can you network better? Can you cut costs? Can you save on taxes?

There are a million possible solutions to your problem, but you need clarity on the steps needed, and then you need to take action immediately.

Be a *good* householder. It starts right here where you're standing.

It's time.

We're ready to start mapping out your first Gong right now.

YOUR CURRENT SITUATION

I'd like for you to reference your answers from the end of Chapter 2 right now. You listed your current situation in each area of your Garden. Have a look at each list and make sure it's still relevant today. You may have jammed through this book or taken months to get here. Just make sure that what you wrote before applies to the present moment, and then bring it over here.

The Five Areas of My Life Garden

Health
My Current Status in Health

0   1   2   3   4   5   6   7   8   9   10

Please go to theurbanmonk.com/focus to get your overall Vitality Score.

If it's been more than a month since you did this, let's see what changed.

Here's a link to the resources page where I have the Medical Symptom Questionnaire from the Institute for Functional Medicine: theurbanmonk.com/focus.

Filling out both assessments will give you a good idea of where to start in the Health area of your Garden. That said, these quizzes and assessments are a reflection of your health state *right now* and not how you'd like to feel. If it's been a while, it's worth doing them again.

Family and Friends

My Current Status with Family and Friends

0   1   2   3   4   5   6   7   8   9   10

Here are the general questions to answer (for yourself).

Where do you stand with your parents, if they're alive?

Where do you stand with your spouse, partner, or lover?

Your siblings?

Aunts and uncles?

Cousins?

Are you alone and lonely?

Are you surrounded by toxic people?

Where do you stand with your kids?

Your oldest friends?

Your colleagues?

Your new friends from the last few years?

Your exes?

Your pets?

Think about all the people in your life, and do an assessment of how much time and energy you're putting into them. How much Water is going to this part of the Garden? Are you happy with the outcome? Spend some time thinking about it as you fill in this section.

Career

What's the current status of your career? Fill out the following questions, and keep digging if there's more. Really get into it, and make sure you're honest about where you currently stand.

Are you happy and fulfilled with your work?

Are you miserable in your job?

Is your career depleting another area of your life? Which one(s)?

Do you have a plan for where you want your career to go?

Have you mapped out retirement and what that would look like?

Are you terrified that you won't be able to retire?

Do you never want to retire because you love what you do?

I've also compiled some great financial assessment tools for you. Please go to theurbanmonk.com/focus to get access to them. If money is what's sucking your energy dry, it's really important to take a cold, hard look at it. Please do this now.

Passions

We need a strong and solid reason to do the things we're doing. They've got to bring joy and happiness in some way, or it's all a waste of time. Let's draw out some of the things that stoke your passion.

What have you accomplished that you're happy about?

What are you getting to do that nourishes your soul?

Where are you doing things that simply make you happy and fill your tank?

What currently sparks the most joy for you in life?

Thinking about these things isn't a luxury. It's a necessity. Life will carry on, and your time will run out. Why shouldn't you deserve an ideal life? You do.

Desires

Where are you currently at with the things you've wanted in life? It's okay to want things in life, and you can find a healthy balance between material objects and life experiences.

> What's the current state of the things you've got?
> Your car?
> House?
> Toys?
> Jewelry?
> Clothing?
> What have you bought for yourself that you're happy about and proud of?

Again, list anything else that comes to mind right here so you have a good log of where you started. These are not things you *want* but things you currently have.

My Negative and Harmful Memes

In Chapters 3 and 4, we looked at some of the weeds, harmful habits, and mental viruses you might be harboring. Go back and look at what you wrote to see if there's anything else you may have thought of or uncovered since then.

Let's list them, along with the positive memes you want to replace them with.

Here's an example of one:

NEGATIVE MEME	POSITIVE SWAP
There's never enough time in the day	I make time for what's important to me
Money is the root of all evil	Money is energy and can fuel my dreams
Long-term relationships never work	We have what it takes to make this work
I got bad genes from my parents	I can change my epigenetics and thrive
I'm a victim of [x]	I'm in charge of my own destiny

My Life's Purpose

In Chapter 7, you answered a series of questions that were designed to help you think through your life's purpose and to elicit deeper thought and retroflection. Go have a look at what you came up with, and take the time now to take a stab at your Purpose.

My life's purpose is currently _____.

Experiences I'd Like to Have

In Chapter 7, you also did some work about experiences you'd like to have. Have a look and see if anything has changed, and if nothing has changed, bring it all over. Otherwise, add or subtract as you deem fit. You also just jotted some of these down in the Desires section. Here's a chance to consolidate and further think through this list.

The experiences in life I'd like to have are _____.

Things I Want along the Way

What things would you like to acquire along the way? These are material possessions that are somehow fulfilling to you. See what you wrote in Chapter 7, and bring whatever still applies over here.

The material things I'd like to acquire along the way are _____.

My Ideal Life

I'd like for you to write a free-form narrative in your own words about what your ideal life looks like. Just dive in.

Here's an example of mine:

> I live on a ski mountain with my family and dogs. I hike, bike, and ski all year round. I have fast internet at my house, so I can work and create right here in paradise. I make films and series, write books, and create a powerful, positive impact on the world while maintaining balance in my health and affairs. I have time to read and meditate daily and really enjoy the natural world around me. Money flows in abundantly from all directions, and I have the freedom to do projects that inspire me and help make the world a better place.

That's just an example. What does yours look like?

My ideal life is made up of _____.

My Accomplishments

It's important to have positive mental energy about things we've already accomplished in life; it helps to prove to our subconscious that we're already capable. Any negative voices need to be kept at bay in this work, so let's dig and anchor in on the past wins.

A baby learning how to walk is a miracle to observe, and it takes them lots of "fails" before they get it. You did this too. You learned to speak and talk. Start there if you're feeling down. You're a powerfully capable blob of flesh that's somehow able to skip, run, jump, and drive. That's a miracle.

What else have you done that you can feel good about?

The accomplishments I'm proud of are _____.

My Core Strengths

No matter how down and out you may feel right now, there's a ton of good you may not be thinking about. We've all got some core strengths that we can use as assets or tools in planning our first Gong. You may be a great connector of people; you may have good speaking skills; you may be organized and methodical.

List your core strengths so we can reach back and draw on them for your Gong. You may have a real or perceived shortage of resources, but let's tap into your *resourcefulness*. You'll be surprised how much energy lies beneath the surface. You simply haven't seen the value in it yet.

My core strengths are _____.

My Unique Contribution

You are truly one of a kind. From the DNA you came with to the unique signature of your microbiome to the trillions of little experiences that have gotten you to today, there's nobody exactly like you in this Universe. Even identical twins diverge greatly due to environment and experiences. With that in mind, write about what you think your unique contribution to the world could be. Don't worry if you're not sure yet; it's not set in stone. Mine has changed over the years, and from Gong to Gong, I can see my own growth and self-discovery. This is an exercise that'll keep you doing regular introspection and retroflection.

My unique contribution to the world is _____.

My Known Issues

Finally, let's get into the weeds you clearly know about. More will come up over time, but we're all smart enough to know the core ones. Maybe you procrastinate. Perhaps you're very insecure. Maybe you've picked up a habit of lying to yourself and others. It could be anything.

You know this. Be honest and know that whatever you write is yours. Hide it and keep it to yourself if you're ashamed of it. Treat it as a diary that you protect so you can *be honest.* That is what's needed if we want to really change. We have to get real.

The things (weeds) I know I need to work on are _____.

YOUR FIRST GONG

Now it's time to make your plan.

We've assembled the ingredients and examined your life in many ways. It's hard to know where to start unless you work backward. We're going to go out five years—that's the absolute most I think makes sense. Even then, it's a lot of conjecture and dreaming, but it's still a great place to start. If we make a plan for where we want to be in five years, we can establish where we need to be in one year and then drill down to what needs to get done in the next 100 days.

We'll break it up from there and keep drilling down. That said, in my experience, most people are overly ambitious about what they can achieve in five years. They say they will be worth billions of dollars, grow two feet taller, and have perfect health and family balance. That sounds great, and some can get close to that, but again, let's make sure we're being realistic.

It all depends on where you're standing right now. If your current situation is a complete mess, a good start may be perhaps to be out of debt, seeing friends, and on a great trajectory in five years. Life doesn't stop there for most. You keep going. Perhaps you'll eventually reach your long-term dreams in 10–15 years. I don't know where you're starting from, but the point is, be real and make steady progress. This is all about making a *realistic* plan that is actually achievable so we can work toward it daily and *actually get there*.

If you map out your Five-Year Plan and then have trouble trying to figure out what needs to be done in the first year, perhaps you're overreaching. Start with reasonable goals, and make sure you can get there. For example, say my goal is to live in Spain within five years. Perhaps my one-year goal would be to become fluent in Spanish and shift to working remotely from home. We all have certain circumstances. Just think through yours and map it out thoughtfully.

Fill out the section for the Five-Year Plan, and then move to the One-Year Plan. You can make adjustments and refine these goals before you begin. You'll want to stick to your plan once you start your Gong, so before you hit "go," make all the adjustments you deem fit now. Later on, if you find that you pulled your punches in your first Gong, you'll know better and can step it up a bit in the next.

It's critically important not to overcommit yourself in your first Gong so you don't set yourself up for failure. Something as simple as scratching the tip of your nose every day for 100 days can be tough for some people. That's a long time with 100 chances to forget and fail. In fact, doing anything for 100 days straight can be difficult for most of us.

Got it? Let's be realistic and optimistic. Let's remember that life is about the journey, and the destination isn't a real thing. The better we get at living life and enjoying the ride, the easier things get and the more our kung fu improves daily.

There is no end.

You're an eternal being, and this is just the beginning.

The life you think you want is a nice entry point into self-discovery and awakening. As you get better at life, boost your Vitality, get your Life Garden to thrive, and achieve the things that have eluded you, you'll learn a very important thing. You'll learn how powerful and magical you truly are. Then you'll keep creating. You'll keep growing. The paintbrush is in your hand, and you no longer doubt yourself. So what would you like to create next?

MY FIVE-YEAR PLAN

By this date: _____ (5 years from now), I will achieve the following:

These are the super big-picture positive steps I will take to make it happen:

MY ONE-YEAR PLAN

By this date: _____ (1 year from now), I will achieve the following:

These are the big-picture positive steps I will take to make it happen:

Now we're going to take what you need done in *one year* and break that into 100-day sprints. The first 100 days are what's in front of us now. Don't get mired in all the heavy lifting that's to come, and don't worry about the second 100-day sprint or any that will follow. What are the next logical steps you need to take in the next 100 days to get to your one-year goals? That's what I want you to think through and write down in this section.

We're going to do this for each area of your Life Garden. Once you've filled this out, there will likely be some need to adjust it. We may put three or four things down in one area and a couple in another and so forth. When it's all done, there may be too much all together, and it may be unrealistic. But for now, jot it all down, and spend some time thinking it through. You may make a mess of these lists. That's okay. I have fresh versions of all of this for you to download and work on at theurbanmonk.com/focus.

MY NEXT 100 DAYS

For each area of your Life Garden, you're going to set goals for your next 100 days, coupled with the *actions* you're going to take to get there. You can't say "make $150,000" and not drive the sales or flip a house to get there. You can't say "lose 40 pounds" and not factor in the dietary changes and exercise needed to achieve that goal.

If you want results, you tie actions to intended outcomes. You focus attention and then feed it with energy—whether financial, temporal, mechanical, or mental.

That's effort. It's action.

So let's get into it.

The best way to know the date 100 days from now is to simply google it. Figure out when your start day will be for your Gong, and then you can google what day 100 would be. Make sure you count day one in there, so it's usually one day sooner than what Google says—you may want to count it out the first time. Put that date below.

My Next 100 Days
Start Date: _____

By this date _____ *(100 days from your start date), I will have accomplished the following by taking specific actions to achieve my desired goals.*

HEALTH	
Goal	Actions I'm Committing to Take to Get There

CAREER	
Goal	Actions I'm Committing to Take to Get There

FAMILY/FRIENDS	
Goal	Actions I'm Committing to Take to Get There

PASSIONS	
Goal	Actions I'm Committing to Take to Get There

DESIRED OBJECTS	
Goal	Actions I'm Committing to Take to Get There

MY NEXT 60 DAYS

Now that you've completed the 100-day goals, let's dig deeper to see what needs to get done in the next 60 days to get you there. This means taking what's on the 100-day list and either breaking it up or doing chunks of the work to get you there by day 100. Take your list for the 100-day goals and parse out where you need to be and what you need to do by day 60 in order to get where you need to be on day 100. Basically, we're breaking up the 100 days into 30- and 60-day chunks.

An example here would be a 100-day goal of losing 20 pounds. By day 60, perhaps the goal is to lose 14 pounds of it. It would mean increasing your run times, distances, or squat frequency to get there. Perhaps it may mean doing time-restricted feeding and extending your fasting window for the last 40 days after day 60.

Another example may be a 100-day goal of writing a 200-page poetry book. Perhaps by day 60, you'll have gotten to page 150. Again, it's all you. Just think it through and divvy up the work to get there. Do you need to be 60 percent of the way there by day 60? Further? How can you break these tasks up so there's a reasonable and sane path to completion?

Let's do the 60-day goals.

My 60-Day Goals
Start Date: _____

By this date _____ *(60 days from your start date), I will have accomplished the following by taking specific actions to achieve my desired goals:*

HEALTH	
Goal	Actions I'm Committing to Take to Get There

CAREER	
Goal	Actions I'm Committing to Take to Get There

FAMILY/FRIENDS	
Goal	Actions I'm Committing to Take to Get There

PASSIONS	
Goal	Actions I'm Committing to Take to Get There

DESIRED OBJECTS	
Goal	Actions I'm Committing to Take to Get There

30-DAY GOALS

And finally, we're at the most granular level. It's hard to focus on things far out in the future, so let's only look one month ahead now. What goals and actions are needed in the first 30 days to help you hit your 60- and 100-day goals? What specific actions do you need to take in the next 30 days to set the foundation for your Gong? The 30-day goals will feed into the 60 and then the 100. Make sure they flow. Make sure you're being reasonable. All of this together will, in turn, help you set your next 100-day Gong toward your one-year and eventual five-year goals.

Using the weight loss example, perhaps the 30-day goal is to drop the first 5 pounds. This may mean taking actions like long walks, stretching, lifting weights a couple of days a week, or whatever gets the rust out and gets you moving.

In the poetry book example, maybe you make your outline, do some research, pick a style, and set the cadence for writing in the first week, and commit to 20 pages a week for the following. That'll put you through prep and 60 pages by day 30 and put you on a path to get to page 150 by day 60. Does that sound reasonable? Can you write 100 pages in 30 days (from days 30–60) once you've done all the prep and gotten into a rhythm? Perhaps you can. That then gives you 50 more pages to finish and polish off by day 100. This is just an example. Would it work for you? If not, what would? It's your Gong.

You'll have goals for all the areas in your Life Garden, and together, there'll be more things you're committed to. I'm making sure you make realistic goals that are actually attainable. When you've done a few Gongs, you'll get the hang of it and can easily take on more. Please don't go into this all gung ho. I'd love to see you get a solid win under your belt and actually complete a Gong without fail and build from there.

Without fail?

Yeah, that means if you miss a day, you start over. The deal is to do every action item you've committed to without fail for 100 days. We'll fill that part out last. For now, go ahead and think through your 30-day goals.

My 30-Day Goals
Start Date: _____

By this date _____ (30 days from your start date), I will have accomplished the following by taking specific actions to achieve my desired goals:

HEALTH	
Goal	Actions I'm Committing to Take to Get There

CAREER	
Goal	Actions I'm Committing to Take to Get There

FAMILY/FRIENDS	
Goal	Actions I'm Committing to Take to Get There

PASSIONS	
Goal	Actions I'm Committing to Take to Get There

DESIRED OBJECTS	
Goal	Actions I'm Committing to Take to Get There

LOOKING BACK AND MAKING SURE

Once you've written in all your goals for each area of your Life Garden, it's important to go back and make sure you're being realistic. Look at your five-year goals, and then make sure the one-year goals can put you on track to get there. Do the same for 100-, 60-, and 30-day goals. Make sure they make logical sense, and think about all the time needed to complete what you've set out to do. Again, don't set yourself up for failure. You want to prove to yourself that you can win at this. That'll build confidence and momentum for further growth and the development of more and more positive habits.

As you go back and check your work, make sure you understand the Water—the amount of time, money, and energy—it'll take to nurture all these areas in your Life Garden. Spend a couple of days reviewing this, if need be. Read all the sections you filled out in this chapter, and tap into your core strength and accomplishments. Look for possible pitfalls in the weeds you currently see, and take a closer look at your plan. With all you've explored, are there any subtle changes you need to make? Do you need to cancel poker night? Does your kid need a math tutor? Do you really need to get a new car this year? Can you afford to wait and allocate the money toward a more pertinent area of your Life Garden for now?

Once you're comfortable with your plan, it's time to move into the final step.

YOUR DAILY GONG ITEMS

This is where the rubber hits the road. Your daily Gong items are the items you commit to doing without fail for 100 days. They should help you move forward on all fronts with your goals, but they don't need to be overly complicated. Lots of my students start with only one or two items—say, 15 minutes of meditation and one Qigong set a day. That may not seem like much, but it can be very challenging to do for first-timers.

I think the bare minimum for everybody is daily meditation, because it helps power up the part of the brain that keeps us on track and focused. For me, I typically do six- to eight-part daily Gongs now. They tend to include two Qigong sets (morning and evening), meditation, some reading, daily exercise, some dietary practice (like time-restricted feeding), and gratitude.

You can choose whatever you'd like, but be real about it. If you suck at commitments, daily meditation alone is more than enough for 100 days. It's hard enough to start.

If you want to bite off more, go for it, but just know that missing any part of your Gong items means starting over on day one. I've missed days before, and it's no fun. You may want to lie to yourself and make every excuse you can, but alas, a deal is a deal.

Think about what you need most in terms of daily discipline and habit-building, and put it on this list, again knowing that these items are an absolute must on a daily basis.

My Daily Gong items are _____ .

BRINGING IT ALL TOGETHER

Now you have it all down. Congrats!

You've assembled your first Gong and are ready to start. Your daily items are the things you'll need to do every day without fail. If you know you'll be traveling, think it through before you commit or at least before you travel.

For example, if one of your daily items is "swim 10 laps daily," and you travel to a place without a pool, then you're screwed. That said, if you think it through and make the same item "swim 10 laps or do 100 pushups" daily, then you can make that happen in the hotel you're in.

It's a deal with yourself. Half of the learning happens when you learn to plan and do a very important thing for yourself.

You begin to assemble your day—your whole life—around dedicated acts of self-love.

This practice will shift your frame of reference and allow you to make a habit of taking care of yourself *first*. This isn't selfish, not at all. In order to be the person you need to be for your family and community, you need to fill your own tank. The Gong practice will help you to do that.

So you have your daily items. Then you have 30 days to get to your 30-day goals, and so on. These goals leave you room to have some flexibility. You'll quickly learn if you've bitten off more than you can chew. If so, perhaps you can shift the 60- and 100-day goals to accommodate and adapt.

It's okay; learn from it.

You fail if you miss a *daily Gong* item.

You do not explicitly fail your Gong if you don't hit all your 30-/60-/100-day goals. Although I have students who do it that way, I'm a little softer in my approach because over the years I've seen so many people learn and adapt and more successfully and consistently reach their goals. They learn to temper their enthusiasm and better manage expectations of themselves. On the flip side, I've had students that have been too scared to commit to anything. This too becomes apparent in this process.

I don't want you failing over and over.

I want you to have a win.

Of course, the goal is to hit all your goals every time, but that's a work in progress.

The retroflection and lessons learned are key stops on that journey. You'll learn a lot about yourself and break through lots of bad habits. You'll uncover several weeds you were completely unaware of. I promise. Just do the work.

IN SHORT

Get your daily items done every single day for 100 days without fail, or you start over.

Do your absolute best to hit your 30-/60-/100-day goals, and if you don't hit them, figure out what's getting in the way of your success here.

Make sure you're tracking on your one- and five-year goals, and adjust your expectations as you grow.

You'll know your daily items by heart within a few days. As far as your goals go, I ask that you read them daily. All of them! In fact, read through all your Life Garden areas, goals, and Gong every day so you remember what you've committed to and see your weeds and strengths regularly. Many of my students print out their goals and put them in a folder that they review daily. Do whatever works for you. Constant reminders keep us on track.

That's how we home our focus on our goals and manage the trajectory of our lives.

You made these goals, so they can't be complete crap.

If they are, then you need to go back and rewrite them and stop kidding yourself. If this is a deal made with you *by you*, then what gives? You made this plan, and now it's time to stick to it. If you don't like the plan, make a new one in 100 days, after this Gong is over, and learn from your mistakes. That's why I'm lenient on these goals. Most of us are dazed and confused at first, and that's okay; use this time to learn and grow.

Over time you'll get better at this process, and you'll start rocking all your goals. We learn, we grow, we adapt, and we become more self-aware at each juncture and bump in the road.

Each Gong gives us more clarity and more Vitality as we commit to taking care of all the areas in our lives. We water what we choose and watch it grow. If it isn't working, we ask why. We problem solve and keep cranking until we find solutions to our problems. We master the householder responsibilities and free up Water for all the fun things in life.

You've devised a plan and are comfortable with it, and now it's time to start. There will always be a birthday, wedding, weekend getaway, or *something* on the calendar that'll tempt you to wait. That inertia will kill you. I promise you the TV, Instagram, neighbors, or whatever else will draw your focus away and pull you off the work faster than you can blink an eye. The world is riddled with distractions that siphon your attention and suck the soul right out of you.

Run for your life!

You've got an opening right now. All the ingredients are cut up and prepared. You can either make a fantastic meal or walk away and let all the food rot on the counter.

Get to work.

Pick a date in the next few days—ideally tomorrow morning—and *start*. This is the beginning of the rest of your life. It all starts with that scary first step . . .

Take the step.

Start your Gong.

CHAPTER NINE

LIFE AS A JOURNEY

Hopefully by now you've already started your Gong. I'm very serious about the need for urgency and action. It's very easy to get pulled into the humdrum reality that we call the world. Endless distractions are there for us, but don't let them inundate your mind and stun you into inactivity.

The solution to your complex problems isn't more complexity.

Sure, the right information can be helpful, but you already know what you need to do. If there's a gap in what you know, then *specifically* research that, and have that information help you move forward.

For example, let's say one of your Gong goals is to get your blood sugar under control. Great! That's a noble and worthwhile goal that'll help your brain function better and decrease your morbidity and chances of early mortality, allowing you to be here to meet your grandkids.

You may want to research fruits and vegetables that are high on the glycemic index and avoid them. That's a quick Google search away. Don't click on the ads, and look for a reputable publication that's not trying to sell you anything.

Good—that's useful information to you.

Next, you may want to research recipes that use more fiber so you can blunt your insulin response. Check. Perhaps some protein smoothies that fill you up and help you feel more energized . . . herbs that lower blood sugar . . . exercises that help normalize insulin response.

The point is that there's a vast amount of useful information out there—books and articles, blogs and podcasts—that'll help you attain this. Use them. Recruit people and resources to aid and abet you in achieving this goal.

The problem lies in distraction.

You may make the goal as a Gong item and then run across an article that says, "Forget about your blood sugar; your real problem is [x, y, or z]." It may be the aliens or the politicians, the lack of vitamins here or there.

Was your blood sugar high to begin with? Why did you make fixing it a priority? Stay on that. How you get to fixing it can vary with your research, but the proof is in the pudding.

Test it.

In this example, you can check your blood sugar several times a day. People are so caught up in wacky theories nowadays that they've lost their grounding in reality. Whatever you're doing, did it work or not? What moves your blood sugar, and where are the results?

The key is to set your goals and be objective. The millions of distractions out there often ask us to forgo reason. Again, reason is a function of a healthy prefrontal cortex. As you continue to grow and enhance this part of your brain with meditation and mind-body practices, you'll be less susceptible to distractions, but please be mindful and vigilant always.

You are not a hungry ghost. You are awake, alive, and embarking on a mission that will radically transform your life.

BUILDING HEALTHY SOIL IN THE GARDEN

One of the areas that will become more significant to you as you continue this work is the state of your subconscious mind. With better awareness and mindful observation, you'll become more aware of the subconscious programming that's running the show right under the surface. Much like the operating system and various programs "doing their thing" on your computer, you'll notice that there's a lot going on in your mind when you look deeper.

Simple examples of subconscious processes include breathing, your heart beating, and digestion. These things take energy and run all the time without us having to think about doing them. But what about the mental stuff? What about the scripts you downloaded from childhood and beyond? The narratives you've been told that may not in actuality be true?

There are so many experiences from our past that have left a lasting imprint on us. There can be trauma from abuse—both mental and physical. If you've got lots of past trauma, I've created resources for you. I've done an entire series on the subject and have tapped the world's best experts to help my students with this. Go to theurbanmonk.com /focus for resources on this.

For years I'd check my blind spot two to three more times than I needed before merging into another lane due to a previous car accident that sent me spinning off the highway. Fortunately, I walked away and was fine, but the energy of the incident was imprinted in me.

When I was done with my homework as a kid, my dad would chide me for goofing off and tell me to "study more," so I learned to look busy in order to not get yelled at.

For years into adulthood, I couldn't relax. I had to look busy. I took on more than I should have and elevated my stress levels over it. It resulted in weight gain, poor sleep quality, less desire to exercise, and impulsive eating decisions.

I was doing a mind-body practice to relax, all the while fighting a subversive program that kept telling me to get up and stop relaxing. Do you see the inherent problem in that? It's like having a virus running your computer, one that keeps opening tabs and windows while you're trying to shut them.

It took years to find this weed and pull it. It was in the soil of my subconscious. I'd replace it with the positive mental swap of "I deserve to deeply relax and let my body and mind recover. I'm perfectly fine with my accomplishments and will only do better with a little decompression right now."

That was me. What about you?

The key is to find these little things and notice how disruptive and destructive they can be in the grand scheme of our lives.

Keep weeding.

I promise there's hope for you.

TIME AND SPACE

We started with the dissection of certain words we tend to take for granted, like "life," "time," "energy," and "focus." These words carry much meaning, and we're so busy living life that we forget to see how utterly miraculous it is that we can even do basic things—or that we even exist.

Somehow, we humans can have ideas and move matter around us to create things that other beings can see and interact with.

Somehow, we live in this place called planet Earth in the middle of "space," with billions of stars and planets circling all around us, where this particular star we call the sun creates energy that feeds this thing called life on our planet. The plants take rays from the sun and store their energy, and we eat these plants, take that energy, and somehow exist and do our thing.

What is a star? A planet? Where did all this stuff come from? Why? What does it all mean? Does it even need to mean anything, or does it simply exist? Why are *we* here? What's our role?

So many questions . . . so much mystery and room for discovery and exploration.

Then there's the progression of this other axis we call "time." What is that, and why does it exist? Did we just make it up ourselves, or is it a real thing? Why do we show up and then go away? Do we go away? Where do we go? Why? How?

Some of these questions already have answers. We have astrophysics and biology. We have chemistry and quantum mechanics. We have thousands of subspecialties of science with good people looking into these questions and much more. There's so much to know, and we're looking—we're asking and learning. If we don't regress to being primitive apes banging each other over our heads, we may actually evolve into a civilization that continues to advance, grow, learn, and better co-exist.

We're on the verge of tapping into sustainable energy. We already know better when it comes to polluting the planet and living symbiotically with other species; we simply need to change our ways and throw out the regressive "leaders" who are on the take from old industries that are pushing for our collective denial.

We've got work to do, but we have all the tools we need to see it through.

We are conscious creators in time and space and can take things on the mental level and turn them into material reality.

Once you see this, actually *prove* this, in your own life, you'll see that we all have the same innate capacity. The Devil's only power is to convince us that we're powerless so he can tap into our creative energy and use it to perpetuate his own vision of reality, one that looks very much like the world we read about in the news.

It's your power, and it's time to take it back.

As you fuse your attention and intention, your Fire and Water, you create steam. That opens your spiritual centers and helps you see more clearly. As this happens, you clear the cobwebs in your mind and can continue to grow. You pluck the weeds you discover and continue to thrive.

Your soil gets healthier, and your Garden blossoms.

Your life starts working, and you have extra energy to be more creative and effective in your life.

You invest that energy into further growth as you radiate and impact others in a positive light.

You wake up and become a star. Not the Hollywood kind but the kind up above us. Your rays provide energy and clarity to those around you. You are a beacon of enthusiasm and optimism. People can see the transformation in you. You don't need to talk about it, because you *are* it.

That's the difference. Change your life and change your ways, and people can see it. This is the way to lead by example.

Be kind to yourself, and keep working through your Gongs.

This isn't a "one and done."

Keep going. After your first one, pick what's next, and keep navigating in the direction of your longer-term goals.

Things may change . . .

What you think are priorities right now may shift as you continue to grow and wake up.

You've been given this amazing opportunity to somehow be alive on this random planet in the middle of outer space with the innate capacity to dream things up and create them in material reality.

To create.

What's it going to be?

ENDNOTES

Chapter 5

1. Kerry J. Ressler, "Amygdala Activity, Fear, and Anxiety: Modulation by Stress," *Biological Psychiatry* 67, no. 12 (June 15, 2010): 1117–19, https://doi.org/10.1016/j.biopsych.2010.04.027.

2. Laurie Kelly McCorry, "Physiology of the Autonomic Nervous System," *American Journal of Pharmaceutical Education* 71, no. 4 (August 15, 2007): 78, https://doi.org/10.5688/aj710478.

3. J. M. Fuster, "Prefrontal Cortex," in *International Encyclopedia of the Social & Behavioral Sciences*, ed. Neil J. Smelser and Paul B. Baltes (Pergamon, 2001): 11969–76, https://doi.org/10.1016/B0-08-043076-7/03465-3.

4. David S. Black et al., "Yogic Meditation Reverses NF-κB and IRF-Related Transcriptome Dynamics in Leukocytes of Family Dementia Caregivers in a Randomized Controlled Trial," *Psychoneuroendocrinology* 38, no. 3 (March 2013): 348–55, https://doi.org/10.1016/j.psyneuen.2012.06.011

5. Ivana Buric et al., "What Is the Molecular Signature of Mind–Body Interventions? A Systematic Review of Gene Expression Changes Induced by Meditation and Related Practices," *Frontiers in Immunology* 8 (June 2017): 670, https://doi.org/10.3389/fimmu.2017.00670.

Chapter 6

6. Kelsey Gabel et al., "Effects of 8-Hour Time Restricted Feeding on Body Weight and Metabolic Disease Risk Factors in Obese Adults: A Pilot Study," *Nutrition and Healthy Aging* 4, no. 4 (June 2018): 345–53, https://doi.org/10.3233/NHA-170036.

7. David S. Black et al., "Tai Chi Meditation Effects on Nuclear Factor-κB Signaling in Lonely Older Adults: A Randomized Controlled Trial," *Psychotherapy and Psychosomatics* 83, no. 5 (August 2014): 315–17, https://doi.org/10.1159/000359956.

8. Bassam Khoury et al., "Mindfulness-Based Stress Reduction for Healthy Individuals: A Meta-analysis," *Journal of Psychosomatic Research* 78, no. 6 (June 2015): 519–28, https://doi.org/10.1016/j.jpsychores.2015.03.009.

9. Sara W. Lazar et al., "Meditation Experience Is Associated with Increased Cortical Thickness," *Neuroreport* 16, no. 17 (November 28, 2005): 1893–97, https://doi.org/10.1159/000359956; Shin Yamamoto et al., "Medial Prefrontal Cortex and Anterior Cingulate Cortex in the Generation of Alpha Activity Induced by Transcendental Meditation: A Magnetoencephalographic Study," *Acta Medica Okayama* 60, no. 1 (February 2006): 55–58, https://doi.org/10.18926/AMO/30752; and Singh Deepeshwar et al., "Hemodynamic Responses on Prefrontal Cortex Related to Meditation and Attentional Task," *Frontiers in Systems Neuroscience* 8 (February 2015): 252, https://doi.org/10.3389/fnsys.2014.00252.

ACKNOWLEDGMENTS

As always, I'm forever indebted to Dr. Carl Totton for his teachings and mentorship. I'd like to acknowledge the thousands of students who've done this work and helped move this practice forward. My teacher trainers and team have been instrumental in the success and dissemination of the Life Garden work. Thank you all for doing the work.

ABOUT THE AUTHOR

Dr. Pedram Shojai is a man with many titles. He is the founder of Well.org and the *New York Times* best-selling author of *The Urban Monk, Rise and Shine, The Art of Stopping Time*, and *Inner Alchemy*. He is the producer and director of the movies *Vitality, Origins*, and *Prosperity*, and he has produced several documentary series, including *Interconnected, Gateway to Health*, and *Exhausted*. In his spare time, he's a Taoist abbot, a doctor of Oriental medicine, a kung fu world traveler, a fierce global green warrior, an avid backpacker, a devout alchemist, a Qigong master, and an old-school Jedi bio-hacker working to preserve our natural world and wake us up to our full potential. You can visit him online at www.theurbanmonk.com.

Hay House Titles of Related Interest

YOU CAN HEAL YOUR LIFE, the movie,
starring Louise Hay & Friends
(available as an online streaming video)
www.hayhouse.com/louise-movie

THE SHIFT, the movie,
starring Dr. Wayne W. Dyer
(available as an online streaming video)
www.hayhouse.com/the-shift-movie

***

*DODGING ENERGY VAMPIRES: An Empath's Guide to Evading
Relationships That Drain You and Restoring Your Health and Power,*
by Christiane Northrup, M.D.

*THE POWER OF VITAL FORCE: Fuel Your Energy, Purpose,
and Performance with Ancient Secrets of Breath and Meditation,*
by Rajshree Patel

SACRED POWERS: The Five Secrets to Awakening Transformation,
by davidji

All of the above are available at your local bookstore,
or may be ordered by contacting Hay House (see next page).

***

We hope you enjoyed this Hay House book. If you'd like to receive our online catalog featuring additional information on Hay House books and products, or if you'd like to find out more about the Hay Foundation, please contact:

Hay House, Inc., P.O. Box 5100, Carlsbad, CA 92018-5100
(760) 431-7695 or (800) 654-5126
(760) 431-6948 (fax) or (800) 650-5115 (fax)
www.hayhouse.com® • www.hayfoundation.org

———

Published in Australia by: Hay House Australia Pty. Ltd.,
18/36 Ralph St., Alexandria NSW 2015
Phone: 612-9669-4299 • *Fax:* 612-9669-4144
www.hayhouse.com.au

Published in the United Kingdom by: Hay House UK, Ltd.,
The Sixth Floor, Watson House, 54 Baker Street, London W1U 7BU
Phone: +44 (0)20 3927 7290 • *Fax:* +44 (0)20 3927 7291
www.hayhouse.co.uk

Published in India by: Hay House Publishers India,
Muskaan Complex, Plot No. 3, B-2, Vasant Kunj, New Delhi 110 070
Phone: 91-11-4176-1620 • *Fax:* 91-11-4176-1630
www.hayhouse.co.in

———

Access New Knowledge.
Anytime. Anywhere.

Learn and evolve at your own pace
with the world's leading experts.

www.hayhouseU.com

Listen. Learn. Transform.

Listen to the audio version of this book for FREE!

Gain access to endless wisdom, inspiration, and encouragement from world-renowned authors and teachers—guiding and uplifting you as you go about your day. With the *Hay House Unlimited* Audio app, you can learn and grow in a way that fits your lifestyle . . . and your daily schedule.

With your membership, you can:

- Let go of old patterns, step into your purpose, live a more balanced life, and feel excited again.

- Explore thousands of audiobooks, meditations, immersive learning programs, podcasts, and more.

- Access exclusive audios you won't find anywhere else.

- Experience completely unlimited listening. No credits. No limits. No kidding.

Try for FREE!